A High Country Life

TALES & RECIPES FROM A
NEW ZEALAND SHEEP STATION

Philippa Cameron of 'What's for Smoko'

Photography by Dana Johnston and Lottie Hedley

ALLEN&UNWIN
SYDNEY · MELBOURNE · AUCKLAND · LONDON

A High Country Life

To generations of ladies
in the kitchen, the backbone
of rural New Zealand

Contents

Introduction

HERE LIES A TALE from my kitchen window, a window that faces east and watches the sun rise each morning. As I look out across the undulating landscape I often see the dust rise from the sheepyards where the men are working. During shearing I hear music pumping across the paddock from the shearing shed and into the kitchen, where every day without fail I smell the arrival of the easterly at three in the afternoon. At the back door, piles of boots ignore the purpose-built rack and, beyond, my little vegetable garden sits proudly in front of a washing line fashioned from two telegraph poles and fencing instruments. Each year my garden teaches me more about the climate here at Otematata Station, a 40,000 hectare high country station in Otago where we are the fifth generation to farm. No matter the season, my kitchen is a hive of activity. With our girls Flora and Evelyn underfoot, eager to help mix icing or more importantly get the first lick of the spatula, there is often a batch of smoko on the go. Dirty bowls sit on the bench waiting for the sink to fill, and despite sweeping the floor regularly there is always the slight crunch of sugar beneath my shoes. Standing at the sink in front my window I can often be found looking out over the landscape, reflecting on the seasons as our family and farm continue to grow.

OPPOSITE: My kitchen window, adorned with freshly bottled fruit and a collection of horseshoes that the children have found.

OTEMATATA STATION IS A high country station situated in the Waitaki Valley, in the lower half of the South Island. A pastoral lease, it comprises the lowlands that border the small North Otago town of Otematakau, commonly known as Otematata, and stretches over elevated terrain all the way to the Hawkdun Range. Once a remote farming area, Otematata is now a busy summer spot after the construction of two hydro dams on the Waitaki River created the Benmore and Aviemore lakes. The original farmhouses, which relied on the house cows Molly and Daisy for their daily milk, are now near the Otematata township, where a bottle of milk is not far from the bottom of our driveway and the house cows are long retired.

With the station's highest point being 1876 metres above sea level, snow is present throughout the seasons — a view that is sadly obstructed by a range behind our house. Beyond those hills there lies a valley that is the gateway to the remote landscape that defines the property. It's a sparse environment completely at the mercy of the elements, with blankets of rich golden tussocks that breathe with the winds, and deep gorges gouged by rivers over millennia.

Otematata Station's roots go back more than a century. My husband Joe Cameron's ancestors, Hugh and Sarah Cameron, first purchased the land holding named Aviemore Station in 1891. In 1908 two of their twelve children, Joesph Farrar and Walter Preston, purchased an additional larger run holding named Otematata, and combined the two properties. When Joseph passed away in 1924, Walter took on the management of both the run holdings from his farm Wainui near Kurow, where he and his wife Frances had four children before she sadly died when her youngest was only six years old.

During World War Two, Walter moved to Otematata Station and oversaw the operation of all the properties. When his second son Robert returned home after serving in the Air Force, he took over management of the Wainui

OPPOSITE: Looking out across Lake Benmore, Loch Laird and Lake Aviemore. Otematata Station is in the background.

property, and Walter stayed on at Otematata. Then in 1950, when Walter retired, his youngest son Joe took on management of Otematata Station along with the newly acquired Awakino Downs, a property near Kurow, completing the 40,000 hectare enterprise.

Joe and his wife Mary were the first generation to raise their children on Otematata Station, but the third generation to farm it. The only son of their three children is my father-in-law, Hugh. My husband Joe (the pool of Cameron men names is shallow) is the eldest child of Hugh and Mandy, and brother to Olivia, who works as a radiographer in Christchurch with her husband Dan and gorgeous children Poppy and Hugo.

While Joe grew up on the station, he was always encouraged to chase his dreams further afield. And he did. Joe has a passion for flying, and gained both his fixed-wing and helicopter licences at an early age. After his OE he later gained employment with the airline Jetstar, which saw us stationed in Melbourne and Christchurch. We would often discuss moving home to the station and farming, and both agreed that's where we saw ourselves raising our family, continuing his family's stewardship of the land.

In 2015, when our first daughter Flora was six months old, Joe resigned from his job and we sold our house in Christchurch. We packed up the horse truck and moved to our newly renovated Twizel cottage on the farm. A Twizel cottage in the Waitaki Valley is a lasting footprint of the hydro-scheme development in the sixties. This was the start of our next chapter in life, as farmers.

The career change has not come easily for the two of us. Joe misses aspects of flying, and I miss my old job as a teacher. But what it has done is forge a path for our future. Watching Flora and her little sister Evelyn (who joined our family twelve months after the move) lie in the sun peering through gaps in the old wooden bridge over the Clearstream looking for trout, or hearing their squeals and giggles as they attempt to catch and pat a chicken, you know there isn't a more enriched environment we could raise our children in. It's also one that ensures we are able to come home to each other at night, a luxury our past careers would not have afforded us.

We want our girls to grow up in an environment that fosters ingenuity, integrity, good work ethic and respect. We want them to be active and respect the land they are privileged to have a connection with. Most importantly we want them to become lifelong learners. To me these values are synonymous with being a country kid — they're also values that Joe and I have been surrounded by our whole lives.

OTEMATATA STATION IS PREDOMINATELY a merino sheep farm, where 30,000 sheep roam the expansive land. The merino is a breed originating from Spain, known for some of the whitest, finest and softest wool of any sheep, making it suitable for 'next to skin' and outdoor apparel, fine suiting and even shoes. Wool is a wonder fibre. It's fire-retardant, hypoallergenic, odour-resistant, breathable, sustainable and compostable — meaning it comes from nature only to return there with a minimal footprint. I especially enjoy wool as my first layer against the skin; a smooth merino singlet is a far cry from the itchy woollen singlets I remember as a kid. You may have some of Otematata Station sitting in your dresser, hanging in your wardrobe or even resting on your shoe rack: we supply wool to contracts including Icebreaker, Reda 1865, Allbirds, Mons Royale, Aclima and Smartwool.

We sell through The New Zealand Merino Company (NZM), a grower-owned group that markets merino wool, which can fetch six to ten times the price of strong wool. In 2007 Otematata Station was accredited by NZM's ZQ brand, representing quality, environmental sustainability, animal welfare and social responsibility. We are strong supporters of the ZQ ideals and, as we build up a team of employees who share the same values as us, Joe and I have an opportunity to honour our obligations to NZM and more importantly secure a strong future for our girls and for farming.

The station is also home to 500 head of cattle (Hereford cows that are

mated with Angus and Hereford bulls) who also enjoy what the rough country has to offer. Where the merinos don't thrive, the cows do their best. They eat the pasture down in the gullies that the sheep can't get to and help to manage the land. Each morning as the sun takes its time climbing above the steep terrain, you can see the steam rising from the cows' warm bodies among the ever-persistent briar bushes. The bright red of the rosehip berries contrast with the rusty red of the cattle. I'm not sure who is more content in that environment — the cattle or the musterer.

LIKE A BRAIDED RIVER, a rural theme has interwoven my life, streams of friends and family influencing my path. My grandmother Vyna was the daughter of a station cook and a horse-broker/blacksmith. She and her seven siblings grew up on Glenaray Station in Southland, where she eventually met and married my grandfather, Archibald. My grandad was just thirteen when he left school in 1938 and began shearing. He was the epitome of a high country musterer: tall, strong, rugged, swore like a trooper and fuelled by my tiny and petite grandma's hearty cooking. I remember as a girl placing my hand in his palm and being encompassed by the enormity of it. Even as a young adult my hand still could not fit.

I am the youngest of my sisters. We grew up rurally in the small town of Herbert, North Otago. My dad was a plumber and my mum, who trained as a nurse, started a piggery business while also working as the local school bus driver — jobs that allowed her to be there for us before school and again when we got home.

Herbert was a great little town to grow up in, with a thriving school and rural community. Summers were spent in the river, and I biked the several kilometres to my friends' houses to play. But terms such as 'succession' and

OPPOSITE: My husband, Joe, doing pre-flight checks
on the Hughes 300 farm helicopter.

'generational farming' were foreign to me growing up on our seven acres. My two elder sisters were never excited by the rural lifestyle, and neither returned to the country after studying. I, however, would always be out and about. I'd be down the back paddock making fires of little scraps of wood and popping potatoes in tinfoil to bake in the embers, or biking down the road to check on calves for our neighbour Mr Pile. To Mum's horror, my first driving experience was in a truck at age ten, moving it back to our house from one of the paddocks Dad was making silage in. I remember explaining to Mum that it was okay, I'd only used first and second gear like Mr Saxton, one of the locals, had told me to.

I was just nineteen when I first worked on a high country station as a wool handler for a shearing gang. Throughout my twenties I spent summers between teaching terms working in tailing gangs on some of the most remote Central Otago stations, and even nannied for a family in Lindis Pass. I was drawn to the remote and isolated beauty, and made so many friendships along the way. When I was 25, I cooked on a large Western Australian grain farm during a seeding season and was mesmerised by the contrast: dusty red earth replaced the familiar steep gullies and snowcapped mountains I knew so well. But what remained constant between stations was the people — the community, and their love of the land over generations.

When Joe's mum Mandy passed away in 2017 and I inherited her job — one that doesn't have an official title but sure has a lot of roles (the main being station cook) — it wasn't my family I called on in the early days for those tried and true recipes, but rather my farming friends who I've known forever. My friend Bec Calder from Lauder Station, who I adore and relied on through sewing and boy emergencies in my early twenties, was the first to share her trusted mousetrap recipe. And from there I began to compile recipes that were quick to make, used minimal ingredients, and stood the test of the old musterers. You know it's a success if the tins come back empty.

'SMOKO', TRADITIONALLY A TERM used to describe cigarette breaks in a working day, is now used in farming to mean morning and afternoon tea. Even though some still stop to roll a cigarette, the majority take the time to grab a cuppa and a handful of something tasty to fuel their bodies.

Depending on the time of year, I cook smoko for our shepherds and staff ranging from three to ten people. Some days, if they are out on our remote high country blocks, or are busy at our property near Kurow, I will also prepare a lunch. Each day is different, depending on the time of year and when we are busiest: shearing in spring, lamb marking in summer and the muster in autumn. There once were cooks employed on the station who lived in the cookshop and served three meals a day plus smokos. But as the farm has evolved, and farming practices have become more automated, we no longer need to employ such a large staff and so the cook's job fell to the willing wife.

With two small girls at home I am glad of the opportunity to earn a little pocket money, but I also want to promote positivity in the role that so many of us who marry into farming families find ourselves in. It's not always easy,

ABOVE: Arthur Cameron, Jim Smith, Vic Hathaway, Isy Cochrane,
Hugh Cameron, Bob Cameron and Marion Cameron enjoying
smoko in a field of oats at Wainui, 1926.

and I do find the days long when juggling looking after the girls and cooking. It can mean early morning starts and late nights on my feet, squeezing in baking between adventures with the girls, travelling the 30-plus kilometres to kindy and further to the big smoke for groceries. But this job allows me to be present in my girls' lives and enjoy the small amount of time I have with them before they begin school.

As I've taken on the role of the cook, I have found a purpose in it. Some may feel that being tied to the kitchen is a step backwards for feminism. But I see my role as important. Some days it may seem like just a cuppa and a scone, but it's more than that. It's bringing everyone together for a yarn or a debrief, and when the staff might include young people who haven't long left home or others who are new to your sector of farming, it's important to provide a space to sit and relax, ask questions or share a joke. Otherwise, it could be a long and lonely day out on the hill or working in the yards. Smoko is not only fuelling bodies but caring for wellbeing.

So even though I may have left my career behind me, I am enjoying the journey of this new one. It's a privilege to be involved with farming this idyllic high country property, one I get to share with my children and my best friend.

THROUGHOUT THE BOOK you will find seasonal recipes that work well at different busy times on the farm. I hope you find these simple and adaptable recipes not only great for feeding farmers, but for feeding families or shouting your workmates hearty and filling food.

Over the course of my farming journey I have also learnt and invented many a life hack that I now can't live without. When you live remotely, some days you have to be resourceful and keep a few tips and tricks up your sleeve to get you through. At the back of the book you will find a list of my best

OPPOSITE: Stopping for smoko in the
paddock near Parsons Rock Spurs.

suggestions for time-saving tricks and little shortcuts. You don't have to live on a farm to make use of these tips; they are for busy homemakers who love a good life hack.

One way that we at Otematata can continue our relationship with this land is to begin to live more sustainably. I like to do one thing — just one thing at a time — towards a sustainable future here on the farm, ensuring that we are role models not only for our own children but for the next generation. Whether it is subscribing to a plastic-free toothbrush service, creating a home compost to improve our vegetable garden, or perhaps finding a service to pick up and process our farm plastic waste, we want to care for the environment by being at the forefront of positive change in home and farming practices.

I hope that you — a seasoned high country cook, an urban mother or anyone in between — are able to gain a little something from the pages that follow. I like to imagine you sitting down with a cuppa at smoko with other readers, chatting and swapping new recipes and tricks, or simply gaining a better understanding of your neighbour — between the city and the country, finding common ground through our kitchens and our values.

THERE ARE DAYS WHEN bowls are stacked in the sink and floury handprints are smeared on my jeans, and there are days when I lose track of time and need to conjure up some smoko quickly. But when the easterly dies down in the evening and the twilight hours begin, I wander out into my little vegetable patch and take in the quiet. I water the seedlings and feel revived. It's a time to think and reflect on the day, and plan what to make for smoko tomorrow.

OPPOSITE: A full watering can is hard for Flora to lift.

FOLLOWING: The vegetable garden beginning to grow, with promises of potatoes, tomatoes and other produce.

About my recipes

WHEN I BEGAN TO COMPILE my favourite recipes to share with you I wanted to make sure they were adaptable and fail-safe, so that it wouldn't matter if you were feeding a team of hungry musterers, shouting the team at calving time or taking a plate to your office.

Don't worry if you don't have the kind of cheese that I'm using — adapt and use what's in your fridge. Most of my recipes are made with pantry staples, and each recipe includes a few tips and tricks that I have picked up over time.

Here's just a little housekeeping before you begin:

- I use New Zealand standard measures: a 5 ml teaspoon, a 15 ml tablespoon and a 250 ml cup.
- I like to use the fan-bake setting on my oven because it's designed for even cooking. If you don't have fan-bake or you prefer to use the conventional setting, you may need to increase the temperature by 10–20°C. All ovens are different, and you will soon get to know what works best for yours.
- Make sure to heat your oven to the required temperature before placing your baking inside. Use the middle shelf of your oven to ensure even heat distribution (this is particularly important if you're not using fan-bake).
- All timings are approximate — keep an eye on whatever you've got cooking, as it may be ready sooner or it may need a little more

OPPOSITE: Freshly baked apple pie, made with my
Apple Pie Filling (see page 192).

time depending on your oven. Things you can do to check that your baking is done include:

- **Look at the colour.** You want an even matt colour across the surface of your baking. A shiny surface means the batter is still raw.
- **Press on the surface.** You want it firm to touch, but with a slightly springy texture. (Be careful not to burn your finger.)
- **Insert a skewer.** If the skewer comes out sticky with batter clinging to it, more time is needed. You are looking for the skewer to be clean when you draw it out.

- Don't be restricted by your cake tin and dish sizes. The sizes I have specified in the recipes are just what I have in my kitchen — give the recipes a go with the sizes you have and adjust your cooking time to accommodate for a more shallow dish (less time needed) or a deeper dish (more time needed).
- It was tricky for me to specify the number of serves, because musterers and shearers will consume a lot more than someone at a workplace morning tea! Mary's Sultana Cake may last a week at your home or feed 20 as a plate at a function, but I've seen that same plate come back empty after a day of mustering. It's all relative to who you are fuelling. Instead I have given (for example) the number of slices I would typically cut from the cake.
- When it comes to seasoning, all measures in my recipes are to taste, unless I've given a specific amount.

You'll find a list of my essential items for the pantry and kitchen on page 240, and for some general tricks to have up your sleeve turn to pages 243–260.

OPPOSITE: Little hands can't resist warm bread rolls.

Spring

Shearing time

In August I begin to write lists. I love that feeling of accomplishment when you put a big cross through each task as you complete it. Lists on my phone or computer don't give me the same satisfaction, so I stick to pen and paper. The lists I write at this time of year help me get my head around what needs to be achieved before shearing begins.

When exactly the gang arrives is dependent on a run of fine days and clear mustering conditions, but it usually ends up being the end of August. Over twenty people employed by our shearing contractor descend on the station, and stay with us on and off over the next three months in the shearers' quarters at the head of the driveway. Shearing contractors are known for their progressive attitude towards employment, and do not discriminate on race, sexuality, gender or age. So from year to year a great mix of people pull up our drive with a dust cloud billowing behind them. They reverse their vehicles up

PREVIOUS: Flora and Evelyn feeding Sprinkles and Ice Cream.

OPPOSITE: Rhys Seymour shearing a hogget with control and ease.

ABOVE: Walter Cameron (standing) and Tommy Cairns with a load of wool on a horse-drawn dray at the Aviemore woolshed, which burnt down in 1941.

to huts allocated based on experience and hierarchy, to unpack everything from bedding to heaters and TVs. Last year I even saw a clothes dryer.

The shearers' quarters are a collection of little buildings and farm cottages that have been shifted to the top of the driveway over the years. They range from mud-brick buildings built by the farm's first proprietor in 1860 to newer, more sturdy corrugated-iron dwellings. They all have electricity, and some even have fireplaces. At its busiest the space can sleep 27 people across six sleeping huts, some with three or four rooms and some with rooms to accommodate couples. There's a shower and toilet block, and a large kitchen and dining room with a colour scheme of pastel greens and yellows.

It takes a few days to work our way through the buildings. During the winter months the water to the quarters is shut off to avoid pipes freezing, and so one of the first jobs once the water is turned back on is to check that all the taps and toilets are running properly. It's important to check this early as our nearest plumber is more than 100 kilometres away.

Armed with lunchboxes, bikes and colouring activities, in the weeks leading up to shearing my girls and I head to the quarters to cross jobs off my list. Each little house or cottage gets a sweep and a mop, and each mattress protector gets thrown in the washing machine and hung on the ten-metre-long line. I cross my fingers that the sunburnt pegs will withstand the weight of each white sail as the wind whips them around. It's not uncommon to have to go and find one or two in a nearby paddock. There is often bribery involved for the girls' good behaviour and extra treats for keeping off the freshly mopped floors.

I can't deny there aren't grizzles. I know that I could work a lot faster on my own, but unfortunately I don't have that luxury. Flora Mae and Evelyn Alexander are my two little sidekicks, a permanent fixture at my side. I love having my preschoolers at home with me, but getting things achieved in a timely manner can be quite the challenge. I love hearing their wee conversations when they make up games and play out different scenarios, like when they pretend to be horses. They build horse jumps from fallen sticks and branches, and can be heard neighing loudly as they leap over each one. Already they have found ways to combat boredom together — the friendship that is developing between them is enviable, one I never had with my siblings due to bigger age gaps.

This year each shower got a new curtain and I picked up some great carpet off-cuts at a flooring shop in town, which I had edged for some of the living areas. Tucked in beside the clay hut is an old water tank turned on its side which poses as a woodshed. Joe usually helps me fill and stack it, along with the wood boxes in the huts that have fires.

One of the rooms that the gang fondly calls the party room, where younger members drink and play music after work, consists of mismatched armchairs and couches. Some of these I picked up for free via a local community noticeboard before last year's shearing began. With no visible springs poking out or years' worth of beer soaked into them, they were the perfect pieces for tidying up the room and meant some older pieces could be replaced.

Before the gang arrives I always make sure to warn the local shop of our shearing start date so that they can stock up on cigarettes. On average the shop sells 26 per cent more cigarettes than in a normal week. The local pub also does a good trade.

ONCE THE QUARTERS HAVE been cleaned and dates have been set, it begins. The cook arrives first to set up, and then the gang arrives in convoy. The gang has been on the road and away from home for nearly three months already. Some have come down from the North Island after the main shear and are away from their families this whole time. The pay is good and the work is reliable, so it's worth the time away.

Our gang contractor, Adrian Cox Shearing, has been at Otematata Station since 1987. The story goes that just before he died my husband's grandfather employed Adrian. On hearing the news of Joe's death, Adrian approached

Hugh (my husband's father) and asked whether Hugh would still like him to come. Hugh replied, 'You better bloody still be coming, as I have no one else,' and so the relationship between contractor and overseer began.

It's a bit of a joke between one of my best friends Deb and me, as to who our shearing contractor is. When I was in Dunedin at Teachers' College I would travel to Alexandra, where my mum was living at the time, and would rousey (work as a wool handler) on the weekends and holidays. I loved spending time in the sheds, and the contractor I worked for — Peter Lyon Shearing — would send me to sheds all over the South Island so that I could see different farms and learn about different types of wool. We would leave the base at five-thirty most mornings, and before the first shearing machine was turned on we would have travelled to some of the most beautiful and remote parts of New Zealand. When others were sleeping, I was in awe: a morning's trip might take us around the edge of Lake Hawea on a precarious track blasted from the rockface in to the Dingle, or down to the incredible twelve-stand shearing shed at Nokomai Station in Northern Southland. Over this time I became good friends with Peter's daughter Deb, who eventually was one of my bridesmaids. When Joe and I married, we borrowed a couple of Peter's vans as courtesy coaches and to help transport the catering staff. Deb and I often talk about the moment when Mandy, my soon to be mother-in-law, turned to her and declared that this would be the only time that a Peter Lyon Shearing van would be up the drive, as her loyalty was with Adrian Cox. And so the joke continues now that although she may be our elder daughter's godmother, she still isn't our shearing contractor.

Shearing gangs often get a bad rap for their behaviour or antics, and I'm sure that like anyone they know how to have a good time. But in our experience, once the first handpiece is picked up at the start of the day, the gang are on-task and do an amazing job preparing our wool for our contracts and wool sales.

OPPOSITE: (Top) Wayne Mosen pulling out a hogget.
(Below) Rhys Seymour, Osborne (Oz) Gemmell and Buck Howden.

A shearing gang consists of shearers, wool handlers, the classer, sheepos, the presser and most importantly the cook. The cook fuels the team five times a day, and has to improvise with limited ingredients and an endless supply of mutton.

Our woolshed is more than 120 years old in parts, with additions and modifications made over the years. The old meets the new at the point of entrance, where the rough stone masonry wall contrasts with the cold corrugated iron. At the top of the ramp your senses are invaded the moment you open the door — the smell of wool, the constant hum of the shearing machines, the bark of dogs ringing out from the yards. Music thrums above it all as you take in the intensity of the work at hand. At first glance you might think it's a little chaotic, but it's quite the opposite.

Our shed has eight stands (although I have never seen the eighth ever used), each with an electric shearing machine suspended above it. The type of shed is called a closed board, meaning it is long and narrow — an inconvenient space for a wool handler. I've even mumbled a few curse words myself when I've arrived at a shed and seen a closed board. Imagine working for eight hours in a long hallway of a house, occupied by six or seven people and two more with brooms. The wool handler has to give way to the shearers as they

work, but still carry fleeces back to the table before another shearer finishes, all the while dodging other wool handlers sweeping the floor. If you don't make it back to the shearer in time and they pull another sheep out on top of the fleece, it can inconvenience the shearer, who is paid per sheep — and you, who now owes the shearer a box of beer.

When we shear the ewes we use only six stands because the shearers are faster, and six is a manageable number of shearers for the wool handlers to cope with. When we shear the wethers (castrated rams), an extra shearer is used to keep the quantity of wool coming off the board consistent. The shearers are slower with wethers; they have to be more careful as there are horns and a penis to navigate, plus the animals are bigger and stronger.

The shearer has the job of carefully removing the wool from the sheep. As they shear, they need to do so in such a way that it keeps the fleece complete so that when it is later thrown on the wool handler's table it looks like a template for a sheep's body. Each shearer has their own rhythm when they approach

OPPOSITE: A team of contractors from Austranz Shearing operating the shaft-driven shearing machines in 1957.

ABOVE: A Bedford truck being used for wool transport outside the Otematata woolshed, 1957.

the pen, the sheep and their handpiece. Their movements are powerful, yet careful and are mesmerising to watch.

As the years pass by and the girls get older, I find that they have become more and more interested in watching the shearers. They love standing out of the way by the smoko room door and are spellbound in particular by Wayne, a muscular yet slight man who shears here each year and occupies the first stand. Each movement is smooth and well rehearsed — a shearer might do more than 200 sheep per day.

Each shearer's stand has a pen behind it called the count-out pen. At different times throughout the day the pen is emptied into a larger pen by the shepherds and their tally is recorded, and when the last handpiece is turned off for the day the tally book is added up. This is one of the few times throughout the year that an accurate tally can be taken of the entire flock. That is, of course, if the muster went well and none were left behind. It's also a way for us to monitor the shearers' technique and make sure that they aren't rushing and causing harm to the sheep.

Once there are enough sheep to fill the drenching race — a narrow lane that helps keeps them calm — the Huntaway's bark rings out and the sheep file in to get their dose of drench, a combination of medicines to combat stomach worms. The sheep then run out down the ramp through a shower of dip to help deter fly strike, lice and ticks. Fly strike is when maggots like to feast on bums covered in poo. Last year the sheep also ran through a bath to help combat footrot, a hoof infection.

Once the sheep are mustered and in the shed, it's a bit like that one time a year when you take your dog to the vet to get its feet clipped, and the vet says, 'While you're here let's just give them a worming tablet, check their teeth and clean their ears.' Then it's all over for another year.

Good wool handlers move in their own way, and in my eyes are athletes

OPPOSITE: (Top) Wool handler Sharon Lawton concentrating hard as she prepares the fleece for the classer. (Below) Rose Barnett classing the small hogget fleece.

too. They work hard and seldom have time to stand still during each run. Each has a specific job and, on the half-hour, the lead handler will call 'Over', at which they all switch to the next job on the rotation. This keeps everyone alert, so nobody is lulled by a repetitive task.

If you are on the broom, then you are responsible for the crutchings and bellies, pizzle (urine-stained wool), eye clips (short fluffy wool around the eyes and on top of the nose), and any short wool that falls while the sheep are being shorn.

If you are on the table, your job varies at each station as you prepare the fleece for the classer. The fleeces come consistently over the run (the two-hour stretch of time between breaks), and the team is methodical in their technique and high quality of work for the whole period.

When Flora was two, I would bundle her and a very small Evelyn into the buggy with the smoko and head towards the woolshed, where we could hear the music playing. Each run starts when Wayne, the ganger, turns the music on and picks up his handpiece. The music varies each day: anything from pop and country to reggae and heavy metal, depending on the mood of the gang and the time of day. Flora used to think the gang was having a party and affectionately called the wool handlers 'the dancers', a name that has stuck. The wool handlers are predominantly women, and the thought of girls dancing all day long in the shed appealed to our Emma Wiggle-loving daughter.

After the dancers have prepared the wool, they roll the fleece into a tight ball and place it on a ten-metre-long conveyer with an even space between each one. At the end of the belt, each fleece falls onto a circular table that our classer, Rose, will turn until a new fleece is presented.

Rose Barnett is a softly spoken and gentle woman who has been classing at Otematata Station since 2013, and started when our previous classer Colin Wallace retired after 22 years. As each fleece is dropped in front of her, Rose chooses a sample of wool from various places in the fleece. She checks for

OPPOSITE: (Top) Flora and me watching on from the smoko room door. (Below) Riki Martin throwing a fleece on the table, ready to be skirted.

strength, colour and length. With each of those components in mind she then classes the wool into bins, which then get baled and labelled to identify what they are best suited for. One could be an Italian wool suit, another could be a performance jumper for adventure racing, perhaps a pair of sustainable shoes or even moisture-wicking socks. The classed bales either fill a contract or are sold at auction.

I often help run fleeces to the bins for Rose when the girls are helping in the pens or playing tag on the pressed bales, and find myself in awe as she makes her decisions. She is decisive and precise. I can identify the élite and the really terrible fleeces, but give me anything in between and I'll be glancing over to Rose to study her method.

Our wool cheque is our main source of income, which is then filtered into many different facets in the farm business. Rose is one of the most dedicated and professional people I have ever had the pleasure of working with, and we have no trouble trusting her judgement for what is essentially our livelihood.

Earlier I mentioned the sheepo and the presser. These two work together but have their individual jobs as well. The sheepo's main job is to make sure that the shearers' pens are filled at all times. It's all about timing, because they need to make sure they are filling all of the pens but also that they don't let the sheep in through one gate while a shearer has the other side open — this would end in disaster, giving the sheep a one-way ticket onto the board. They also need to check in with the shepherds in the yards to watch for mob changes. You don't want to mix up mobs.

The presser is the classer's right-hand man. After Rose has sorted a bale, she clearly marks the fadge (the name given to the sack that the bale is pressed into) with the type and grade of wool. It's the presser's responsibility to make sure each bale is pressed exactly to 185 kilograms, and to keep up with the demand from the classer. When they aren't pressing bales, they lend a hand to the sheepo. The sheepo and the presser are usually the last to leave the shed, making sure that their areas are clean and organised before the next day begins.

With an average of 700 bales of wool pressed each shearing, there are always plenty lined up to be loaded onto the truck. If the presser gets each line just right, with minimal gaps between each bale, it amounts to endless hours of 'bale tag' for the children. The rules are simple: if you get tagged, you are in; if you lose your gumboot down in between the bales, you won't get it back until the next truck is loaded.

We transport our own wool to the PGG Wrightson Wool Store in Christchurch, using the station's Hino truck and trailer — which means that it's only a few days between lost gumboots.

The last member of the shearing gang, and most definitely not the least, is the cook. The cook keeps everyone fuelled, fed and in line. The golden rule of 'Don't upset the cook' has higher stakes in a shearing gang; it's a long time with poor food if you upset the cook.

The cook is the first up and has a cooked breakfast on the table by half-six every morning. Throughout the day they provide morning smoko, a hot lunch, afternoon smoko and a cooked dinner (with pudding) for all 26 people. The amount of food served each day is phenomenal, and the cook is always inventing ways to reuse leftovers.

We supply the cook with as much mutton as they need for the duration of shearing — usually the equivalent of half a mutton a day. Each year the cook changes depending on what shearing gang they work with, but one cook, Brian, is amazing at using mutton in the most resourceful ways. When Joe would call in to pick up the pig scraps, Brian would often share some of whatever was on the menu that night, such as mutton schnitzel or mutton mince.

Sometimes, when I find it hard to get a mutton roast for our own fridge, I will go down to the shearers' quarters and barter a couple of legs of pork. The gang gets a welcome change to their menu and I get a roast for the family.

We keep two weaner pigs at this time of year, who fatten up nicely and put ham in the freezer for Christmas. They get a big bucket of vegetable peelings and scraps each day from the shearing quarters' cookshop.

Paige, our German shorthaired pointer, also gets noticeably fatter at this time of year. The pig buckets all have lids, so our only guess is that she directs her doe eyes at the cook as they cut up the mutton each night.

WE SHEAR OUR EWES first in early September, known as the pre-lamb shear, so that the mothers-to-be feel the cooler spring temperatures. This encourages the ewes to take their newborn lambs to shelter when it gets cold. If they still had their fleece on they would not consider the lambs' size-to-wool ratio, and the lambs would not do as well.

The merino are a wary bunch, and so we leave them to lamb in peace, not intervening like farmers of other sheep breeds do. The risk of interrupting lambing is that a ewe might run away, leaving the lamb to fend for itself. We keep an eye on them from afar and do our best to help the survival rate by eradicating pests such as wild pigs who prey on vulnerable mothers and lambs.

ABOVE: Wool being loaded for sale
outside the Aviemore woolshed.

Once the ewes are shorn we have a break of a fortnight, which gives the shearing contractor a chance to finish pre-lamb shearing on other properties before coming back to shear our ewe and wether hoggets. Ewe hoggets aren't shorn with the ewes at pre-lamb because they are essentially only one year old, which is too young to lamb.

Not many farms keep a wether flock like we do, as it's better to utilise their space with breeding ewes or fattening lambs, but we can keep large numbers of them because we have extensive high country. The wether flock is purely kept for their wool properties. Their wool is not as fine as the average ewe's, but it is still a high-quality product.

I have a soft spot for the wethers. They are like little hermits who have minimal human interaction, and when it's time to move anywhere they do it in their own time. It's like getting a group of grumpy old men to move from their favourite armchair to the kitchen for a haircut. After shearing, the wethers are mustered by horse and taken home to the end blocks at the edge of our property near the top of the Hawkdun Range, a trip that can take up to a week. In total the wethers see humans and dogs only twice a year (the second during the autumn muster), and the rest of the time they are happy to roam in one of the most remote and beautiful parts of our station. Not a bad life to live, really.

Community spirit

Each year shearing brings its own challenges. One such was when my beloved mother-in-law — our girls' granny, my husband's number one supporter — died suddenly on 23 July 2017. Mandy had lived and breathed life on Otematata Station for 30 happily married years. I remember my mum saying to me not long after, 'I guess that now makes you the chief cook and bottle-washer.' At the time I wasn't sure what she meant, but we were only a few weeks away from pre-lamb shearing and so I soon found out. I look back on this time and often wonder how I coped.

With two small humans — Flora had just turned two and Evelyn was five

months — and a new role that I wasn't expecting to take on so early or even at all, I remember thinking, 'What other option is there?' So I got busy.

Evelyn became a versatile wee sleeper, sleeping in a reclined old Mountain Buggy we used on farm, while Flora hung out on my back in a carrier. We would cross off items on a list we were writing as we went along. I didn't want to interrupt the girls' routines too much, and so we would return home for lunch and afternoon naps before embarking on more tasks once the girls had gone to bed that night. That particular year my friend Jess Toole, who was working over the hill at Bog Roy Station, helped me clean the quarters with two teenage girls who lived on the station. And all the while, I prepared and dispatched smoko from my kitchen in between trying to process what this new life entailed.

Rural communities big and small have plenty in common, but one thing that stands out is the number of dedicated people who work selflessly behind the scenes to keep community spirit strong. After Mandy passed and I found myself in the deep end during shearing season, the Food Fairies appeared with a package of baking to pop in the freezer to help with future smokos. These small generosities become life-saving moments.

The Food Fairies is one of my favourite community initiatives. They're a group of mums who cook meals and provide baking to new mums in the area. When Evelyn was born we received the most amazing food package from the families at the Omarama Playcentre, and it inspired me to start a similar group in the lower Waitaki Valley.

The Fairies rely on word-of-mouth, and whenever the stork lands with a new baby we jump into action. We also look after anybody who is enduring a loss. The group doesn't discriminate: whether you live in the village or on a farm, if it's your first or fourth child — everybody deserves to be treated with kindness. Contributions can be anything from a meal to baking, fresh veges from the garden, fresh eggs, homemade preserves or even a store-bought

OPPOSITE: Excitement all around
while feeding lambs on the lawn.

item. It doesn't matter, as long as that family gets a break from having to plan tea, or smoko, or what to put in the kids' lunchboxes the next day. The items are collected in unnamed containers so there's no pressure for the recipient to return them or to say thanks to people they might not know, for those who find those things awkward. It is such an incredible feeling, dropping off the boxes of treats and seeing the faces on the recipients.

Since having the girls I've been a part of several committees, in some cases taking on presidential and secretarial roles. I can't complain about a lack of opportunities for our family in the area if I haven't also taken it upon myself to be useful somewhere. In a small community you do often see the same faces on each committee, and I can only imagine how the community would thrive if we had more diverse voices at the table. Everyone is busy, but perhaps if one member of each household volunteered on a committee, there wouldn't be a need for some to take on too many roles; everyone would be less busy and have more time for their families.

I once read a poem which implied that people who say they are busy shouldn't, because everybody is busy and it shouldn't be a competition to see who has done the most. I disagree, and I often use the word. Of course we are all busy, doing things for our families, farms, workplaces, schools and communities. And of course we are allowed to say the word 'busy'. Even if someone boasts about how much they've achieved in a day, we should congratulate them. They must feel so relieved to have crossed everything off their list!

With such a huge focus on mental health in rural communities at present, we need to be looking for signs of when to help our friends. Using the word 'busy' could be a way of asking for help. I love when my friends ask if they can do anything to help. Could they pick up a child from sports practice or school? Collect something in town to avoid an extra trip? We should be listening to our friends when they say how 'busy' they are. It's not boasting;

OPPOSITE: Filling chocolate eclairs with vanilla instant pudding for shearing smoko.

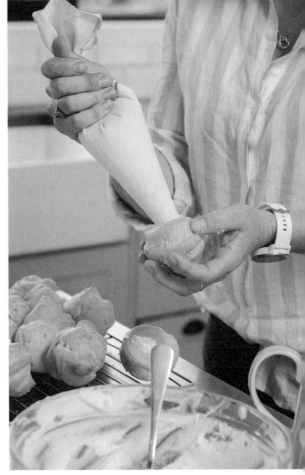

more often than not, they are just saying how hectic their day is. A friend offering to help could be all they need to feel valued and cared for.

Looking back on that year that Mandy passed, I was lonely. A once bustling and busy dam town, Otematata is now a summer holiday or retirees' spot and only a handful of families live here. We had only been home for a year and a half and were still finding our place in the community. Joe and I would watch the steady stream of cars each weekend coming to give their condolences to Hugh, and think how hard it must be for him to relive such a distressing time. But then I would also feel a sense of longing for just one of those cars to come and visit us. To come and ask how Joe was after experiencing that event he shared with his father. Selfishly I would even yearn for someone to ask if they could lend a hand.

Lifelong friends are a godsend in times like this, and I will forever be thankful for the lengthy phone calls and messages I received. But nothing beats someone calling in for a cuppa, or a friend cuddling your baby while you hang out the washing and get tea on. While living in the city we were only metres from our neighbours or blocks from our friends, but when you live remotely you are separated by kilometres and sometimes hours of travel from your friends.

I learnt to find my feet fast that shearing season. I hit the ground running, and in the depths of night while feeding Evelyn I had to cherish those moments that I'd missed during the day, stealing cuddles and listening to her little snuffles.

At the end of the day, we got there. Shepherds and farm workers were fed, robust go-to recipes were perfected, and my new life on the farm was defined.

Teamwork

While most of us wonder when our next weekend off will be, our girls look forward to shearing season. I secretly do too, loving the hustle and bustle of a full house. The station comes alive. Every dwelling is full; we go from the base staff of eight people to 35, give or take. There is a constant buzz of movement and, when you drive up the driveway at night, it's warming to see every hut and home with a light on. Outside of shearing season I am often the only female living on the property, and so it's nice having a laugh with the girls in the gang and yarning to Rose.

The girls don't just love shearing season for the fact that they see new people and hear party music. It's that this time of year is when they get to be the most involved. One of the downsides to living on an expansive property is that a lot of the stock work is done at least an hour's drive from home. During shearing the girls get to see their dad, grandad and all their favourite shepherds each day at smoko time. They join in the banter and laugh along, even though they are still too young to understand the jokes.

I love watching the girls interact with people they wouldn't normally meet. At first they are shy and don't make eye contact when the dancers say hello, and need me to hold their hands when they walk past the wool handling tables into the smoko room. But after the gang has been immersed in our lives for more than two months, the girls' confidence grows. From helping pop fleeces on the conveyer belt, to stamping down fadges of wool with the sheepo, and even sweeping under the tables; the girls' confidence gets a boost as they learn how to be around new people. They see how much Joe and I value and respect the gang's work, and they learn to do so too.

With so many people on the station at one time, there are bound to be some downsides too. At first it annoyed me, but now I'm prepared. We're on the same water line as the shearers' quarters and, when the shearers finish up for the day at five-thirty, the first thing they do is head for a shower, followed soon after by the wool handlers. We have to wait until more than 20 people have showered before I can run the bath for the girls, otherwise the water is no more than a dribble. And with that many people utilising one tank of water, we are always sure to run out.

Our solution is that, sometimes during the day, we turn off the mains and allow the tanks to refill. That means no washing machine, dishwasher, toilet or showers until the tanks have refilled.

This is also the time of year to check your tyre pressure. The driveway becomes incredibly rutted with the constant traffic, including the coming and going of trucks as we bring home and deliver stock; and of course there's the regular departure of the wool truck. The girls sing the same tune each time we go up and down the drive, whether in the buggy or in the car. It simply goes 'Arrrrgggghhhhhh!' as their voices bump along the horrendous track.

Smoko

For the duration of shearing, each day's routine is the same. As the morning light streams in through the kitchen window, you get a glimpse of the day ahead and what the weather will hold. Paige, whose dog bed is beside the fire, will raise her head in acknowledgement as I head to turn the kettle on. She won't be going far just yet, as she knows I'll stoke the fire and have it roaring with warmth in no time.

The house is still and you'll find me in the kitchen first thing, to get the morning smoko prepped and made before the girls get out of bed. This way we can have breakfast together and get dressed without me rushing them out the door to deliver our staff's smoko to the shearing shed. However, the crafty little critters have learnt that they can be fussy at breakfast, knowing that only a few hours later they will have a buffet of delights in the smoko room. The girls don't often like what I have made for the farm workers' smoko; instead they prefer the cut-up saveloys and pastry from the savouries that the shearers' cook has made for the gang. The dancers often keep aside a saveloy for the girls, and even remember that Flora doesn't have any sauce, which is really sweet of them.

If the weather is fine we load up the old steel-frame double Mountain Buggy that my friend Mischa gifted us when she learnt we were going to have a second. This buggy is like no other farm vehicle and has served three families before us. The flat wire cage underneath can fit a wooden tea-tray

OPPOSITE: Flora on quality control as
she watches Rose class a fleece.

of smoko, or if I need extra space, the hood can hold two baking trays side by side. Without sounding clichéd: they just don't make them like they used to. There is no way that smoko would make it to the shed if I was using my newer buggy (which I use when I'm away from the farm). The new model's tray is now a floppy canvas — I can envisage icing sliding everywhere when going downhill.

I can't wait until the day that I get to pass on that buggy to another farming family and share with them some of the stories that the hard-wearing navy canvas can tell. Mischa boasts that not only can it hold two children, but also two 24-packs of beer side by side around a golf course.

One time at the Wanaka A&P show, when Evelyn was less than two months old, Joe had taken Flora home to have a nap (a perfect excuse to avoid an afternoon of shopping). I walked Evelyn around the stalls while she slept, and ended up lowering the second side of the buggy to pile in my purchases. It got embarrassing when a number of people popped their heads around hoping to see twins, only to find the spoils of my shopping trip.

Morning smoko is delivered at nine-thirty each morning, and Flora set the routine of going to smoko when she was just a year old. Now four years old, she barges up the steps and in through the roller door, announcing her arrival and greeting Rose with a hug. Evelyn, whose motto is 'Me too!', trails behind, bellowing 'Rosie Bunny!' just that little bit louder than Flora to make sure she is noticed too.

Shearing is the time of year when there's a never-ending supply of lollies on the farm, and with the girls being so young I have managed to ration them to two a day. This makes for some hard life lessons: the girls have to ask themselves do they have two at morning smoko, or do they have one in the morning and one in the afternoon. It's like a psychological experiment only it's a daily torment. As soon as we get to the entrance of the shed the girls run straight to Rose, who they affectionately call Rosie Bunny. Even though her lolly jar sweetens the deal, the love is real. Rose spoils our girls and they reciprocate with cards, drawings and blossoms.

After greeting Rosie Bunny the girls then head to the count-out pens to see Dad. If they're lucky, Joe will let them have a lolly from the container that sits next to the tally book, which of course becomes a covert exercise to make sure I don't see. Some days, our shepherd Sarah will sneak one last lolly into their wee hands.

Maybe my own two-lolly rule is counter-productive, but then I often think about a story I once heard from a friend whose little sister used to steal chocolate bars out of the musterer's saddlebags. After a long day in the saddle, the musterer would reach for a sugar hit only to find wrappers in its place. Perhaps sneaking lollies will be a memory the girls share when they are older, about how they fooled the old girl when she wasn't looking. And like any good-humoured mother, I will feign horror.

The lolly jar in the count-out pen is filled with bargain bags I pick up at Rainbow Confectionery in Oamaru. This year the shepherds consumed nearly twelve kilograms of lollies in less than three months. Sarah may point to her sweet-toothed Huntaway dog, but largely the lollies are gobbled up by those who stand waiting to count out the pens.

If Joe is in the shed then the girls and I will join the gang for smoko too. It's nice at this time of day, after an early morning of cooking and then tending to the girls, to actually sit down and have a cup of gumboot tea. The darker the shade of Red Band gumboot-black, the better.

All this ceremony is repeated again in the afternoon, from the walk to the shed to the coercion of lollies, the sharing of smoko and the dark cup of tea. We do this every day for 27 days of shearing; you can see why the girls enjoy the station at this time of year. It's always a big let-down when the last car of the gang rolls out down the drive at the end of shearing.

THE MAJORITY OF MY TIME is spent in the kitchen. I fortunately don't have to feed shearers or staff any lunches at this time of year, like friends of mine do

down the valley. However, it is 27 days of morning and afternoon smokos for seven people (first twelve and then fifteen consecutive days of the pre-lamb and later shearings). By day eight, you begin to question if it's okay to repeat your menu. Of course it is! No shepherd shall ever utter to this cook 'I sure am sick of these mousetraps', or they may just find themselves wearing the cup of tea that I'm cradling after a sleepless night with a teething toddler and her early-rising sibling.

We supply the young shepherds with groceries for their lunches and main meals. However, if the weather has been cold and wet, or if a muster has gone badly (which I can tell from the tone of conversation on the RT radio that sits on top of my fridge), I will make a hot meal and drop it off. When you are feeling a bit deflated, making a fuelling lunch is often low on the agenda — this way I know they will have time to warm up and recharge.

I love the look on the ladies' faces at the checkout when I do the groceries at this time of year. Some of them have known me since I was a teenager and love when I come to their counter, while others cringe at the sight of my two mountainous trolleys. I reduced the trolleys considerably when I started going to the bulk food store to refill my baking containers and getting my flour and sugar from the Farmlands co-op in large quantities (and paper bags). I just couldn't consciously keep putting plastic brown sugar and chocolate chip bags into the rubbish in the quantities that I was. I also like that by buying Farmers Mill flour, I'm supporting a South Canterbury business owned and operated by the farmers who grew the grain. It's the same reason why I buy canola oil farmed and produced by The Good Oil, another successful South Island business. I want to support New Zealand farmers wherever I can in the kitchen.

Last year during shearing I used 25 kilos of flour, thirteen-dozen eggs and lost count of the blocks of butter and kilos of cheese. Quantities and recipes

OPPOSITE: (Top left) Baking essentials.
(Top right) Eclairs freshly dipped in melted chocolate.
(Below) Evelyn and Flora rolling cookie dough for the freezer.

vary from day to day, but the staple ingredients are the same: flour, butter, eggs and cheese.

Each morning smoko I bake one sweet and one savoury option, and in the afternoon they often prefer another savoury item (and clean up the baking tin from the morning). Not all seven staff sit down at the same time, as a couple are often away mustering mobs to and from the shed, so I need options that will last sitting on the table.

That first year of shearing I could hardly make a good scone. My grandma would have called them 'small windowless buildings'. I'm still not a great sponge maker, and not even cream would have disguised the taste of cornflour in my first attempts. As time's gone on I've got better, and now I have a list of fail-safe recipes that act as my go-tos at this time of year.

OPPOSITE: (Top) Flora making herself a Milo.
(Below) My kitchen helper sticking close by so she can lick the bowl once all the eclairs have been dipped.

FOLLOWING: On my way to close the loading door before the girls come in and start playing 'bale tag'.

Pappy's Savoury Scones

Makes 12 scones

2½ cups self-raising flour

2 cups grated cheese

2 eggs

4 rashers bacon

1–2 tablespoons chopped fresh parsley

salt and pepper

1 cup milk

I was given this recipe by Joe's Aunty Katrina, who had been given it by 'Pappi', the shearers' cook here on the station in the early 1980s. Katrina knew it as a muffin recipe, but I gave it a few tweaks and it became a scone recipe. Embarrassingly, though, not long ago I was given Ruth Entwistle Low's book *The Shearers* to read, and as I flipped through the book I saw a chapter about Pappy, a legend in the kitchen, whose recipe I had adapted but whom I had never met. What do you think I noticed straight away? The spelling of her name! I had been spelling it wrong all these years — and for that I do apologise. Whichever way you spell it, though, this recipe is legendary.

Preheat the oven to 200°C (400°F) fan-bake. Line 2 baking trays with baking paper.

Mix all of the ingredients together in the above order — you want the mixture to be quite wet, so you may need a little more milk.

Spoon 6 dollops of the mixture onto each lined baking tray.

Bake for 10–15 minutes until golden in colour.

Tips and tricks

- *I tend to use Colby or Tasty cheese in this recipe, but Edam will work well too.*
- *For a super-tasty variation, add a couple of dollops of relish or a grated zucchini (you may need a little less milk as grated zucchini is very moist).*
- *Leave out the bacon and parsley for a yummy cheese scone.*
- *This recipe can also be made with a gluten-free self-raising flour mix.*

Sweet Soda Scones

4 cups self-raising flour

½ cup caster sugar

1 cup cream

1 cup soda water

I adapted this recipe from the classic lemonade scone, as we never have lemonade in the house but we do have a trusty old SodaStream machine. It's all I use for my sweet scone recipes now.

This recipe is quick to put together and the scones are super soft and fluffy. Once you make scones this way, I bet you will never go back.

Preheat the oven to 200°C (400°F) fan-bake. Line a baking tray with baking paper.

Place all of the ingredients in a large bowl and use a butter knife to gently mix the ingredients together, forming a soft dough.

Tip the dough onto a well-floured surface, and sprinkle a little more flour on top. Use your hands to gently pat down and shape the dough into a rectangle about 2–3 cm (¾–1¼ in) thick.

Cut the dough into a dozen squares, or use a round cutter to make them a little more fancy. Place the scones onto the lined tray, packed tight with a gap of about 1 cm (½ in) between each one — this will help them to rise higher.

Bake for 10–12 minutes.

Tips and tricks

- *If you forget to add sugar (it happens), serve the scones with plenty of butter, jam and whipped cream, and no one will know the difference.*
- *My scone tips on page 70 apply here too.*

Soft and Sweet Date Scones

1 cup chopped dates

3½ cups self-raising flour

½ cup caster sugar (optional as the dates add sweetness)

1 cup cream

1 cup soda water

I think date scones would have to be my favourite type of scone, and these ones are so good that they could even challenge what's on offer in some of the trendiest cafés in the city. They are soft and sweet (as the name suggests), and are best sampled warm out of the oven with plenty of good-quality butter.

I like to cut them in half and butter each side, so that people can eat them straight from the tin while out mustering or in the smoko room.

Preheat the oven to 200°C (400°F) fan-bake. Line an oven tray with baking paper.

Place the chopped dates in a pot, and cover with water. Simmer on a low heat until the dates become soft.

Drain any excess water and let the dates cool as you prepare the scone mixture.

Add the remaining ingredients into a large mixing bowl (in the order listed). Gently bring together with a butter knife, then add the cooled dates.

Tip out onto a well-floured surface, and sprinkle with more flour before shaping into a rectangle approx. 3 cm (1¼ in) high. (Use floured hands to avoid the dough sticking.)

Cut into a 4 x 3 grid to form 12 scones, and place them onto the lined tray, packed tight with a gap of about 1 cm (½ in) between each one — this will help them to rise higher.

Pop in the oven for 12–15 minutes until golden brown.

Tips and tricks

- If you don't have self-raising flour, replace each cup with 1 cup of plain flour and 1½ teaspoons of baking powder.
- As an alternative to sugar, you could add 2 tablespoons of honey to the dates while they are simmering.
- Keep a stash of UHT cream in your pantry to use when you don't have any fresh cream.
- If you don't have a SodaStream, use store-bought soda water or lemonade — but consider purchasing cans that can be recycled easily, rather than plastic bottles.
- If you use lemonade, omit the sugar.
- You could add orange zest to the dates as they simmer for a burst of citrus flavour.
- Scone dough doesn't like to be played with too much. If you use a cutter, make sure to keep your waste to a minimum so that you're not constantly reworking the dough scraps.
- All ovens are different, and the timing may change depending on your scone size. Keep an eye on them — they may need a little longer.

Cheese Rolls

Yvonne's Creamy Filling (option 1)

32 g (1–1¼ oz) packet onion soup

250 ml (9 fl oz) can reduced cream

200 g (7 oz) grated cheese (Tasty, Colby or similar)

Mrs Isbister's Cheesy Filling (option 2)

32 g (1–1¼ oz) packet onion soup

300 ml (10½ fl oz) water

500 g (1 lb 2 oz) grated cheese (Tasty, Colby or similar)

1 heaped teaspoon mustard powder

To assemble

24 slices white sandwich bread (a little more than 1 loaf)

butter

It seems every family has their own version of the classic South Island cheese roll. Here I've given two different options for the filling. The first is my mum Yvonne's creamy version — although many Southlanders have voiced their concern that this is in no way a traditional 'Southland sushi' recipe (they are a passionate bunch)!

The second option comes from Mrs Isbister, who has been a figure in my life for as long as I can remember. I played hockey with her children all through primary and high school, and now I see her most weeks at my local supermarket, where we chat about recipes. Mrs Isbister's version is clearly a good one for scaling up — when I asked her permission to share it, she offered to give me the quantities needed for 230 dozen (an amount they made one year for a hockey fundraiser).

If you are making Yvonne's filling, combine the onion soup, reduced cream and cheese in a pot and cook, stirring continuously, over a low heat. Keep stirring until the mixture is melted and resembles a soft spreadable mixture.

If you are making Mrs Isbister's filling, heat the onion soup and water together in a pot, stirring until it begins to boil. Remove from the heat and add the cheese and mustard powder. (If the mixture seems a bit runny add a handful more of grated cheese.) Let it cool before spreading.

Cut the crusts off two sides of each bread slice using a serrated bread knife (or an electric knife). This makes them easier to roll.

Arrange the bread slices so that the crusts are at the top and bottom and spread the mixture onto each slice, being generous and covering right to the edges. Roll up the slices from the bottom and place them on a baking tray.

Butter each top generously and place under the grill. When they start to brown up, turn over and repeat. Serve hot, with extra butter if you desire.

Tips and tricks

- *Both recipes are easily multiplied.*
- *Strong-flavoured cheeses such as Tasty or Colby work best.*
- *You could also make the filling in the microwave.*
- *I usually set aside a dozen rolls to grill, and put the remaining dozen back into the bread bag to freeze for another smoko, or to pull out for a quick lunch with soup.*

Bacon and Egg Pie

400 g (14 oz) block puff pastry

12 eggs

6–10 rashers bacon, chopped

egg wash or a little milk (optional)

Optional additions

leftover new potatoes, chopped

chopped onions, softened in a buttery hot pan

peas

dollops of tomato relish

Bacon and egg pie is a staple for most busy farmers, but the recipe varies from one kitchen bench to the next. Some people like their yolks left whole, whereas others like them mixed up. Joe refuses onions, but insists on peas, and then there's the question of whether the top should be open or solid . . .

Preheat the oven to 180°C (350°F) fan-bake. Set aside a 32 cm x 25 cm (12¾ in x 10 in) pie dish.

Use a knife to mark thirds in the pastry block. Roll out two-thirds of the pastry and use it to line your pie dish, making sure the pastry goes up the edges. Trim any excess away. Roll out the final one-third, prick with a fork a few times, and place to the side to top the pie with later.

Break the eggs into your dish and use a clean hand to break up the yolks. (I use my hand so that I don't accidentally pierce the pastry with my fork.) Alternatively, if you prefer your yolks whole, leave them alone. Add the chopped bacon and any other fillings you desire.

Place the pastry lid on top and fold down the edges. Use a fork to press down on the edges and seal the pie. Brush with egg wash or a little milk if you want a golden top. Bake for 35 minutes.

Tips and tricks

- *Keep a pair of scissors that you can use specifically for chopping bacon. It saves so much time and hassle.*
- *To avoid the need for tomato sauce — especially if your sauce bottle is in a state after it's been returned from the paddock — drop dollops of tomato relish evenly over the filling before you put the lid on the pie.*
- *Use any leftover pastry trimmings to make a pretty decoration on top of the pie.*

Mandy's Chocolate Cake

125 g (4½ oz) butter

200 g (7 oz) sugar (a teacup)

2 tablespoons golden syrup

½ cup milk

1½ cups plain flour

2 tablespoons cocoa

1 teaspoon baking soda dissolved in 1 cup milk

Chocolate Icing

3 tablespoons cocoa

3 tablespoons caster sugar

3 tablespoons water

3 tablespoons butter

1½ cups icing sugar

When I asked Joe to tell me one of his favourite things that his mum would bake, he chose this cake. So I rang Hugh and asked if he could locate Mandy's well-thumbed, cocoa-stained recipe book. He began to read out the recipe and I realised I knew it! I'd already been using it, but it was penned with a different name in my recipe book. The title in my book has been amended and it is now Mandy's cake.

Preheat the oven to 180°C (350°F) fan-bake. Line your cake tin — I use a 20 cm (8 in) round tin, or a 28 cm x 18 cm (11¼ in x 7 in) brownie tin.

Place the butter, sugar, golden syrup and milk in a pot over a low heat and melt together. Take the pot off the heat and add the flour, cocoa and milk mixture. Mix well and pour into the prepared tin.

Bake for 20 minutes.

For the chocolate icing, place the cocoa, caster sugar, water and butter in a pot and melt over a low heat until the mixture forms a syrup. Sift in the icing sugar while the mixture is hot, and stir to combine.

Pour the hot icing over the cooled cake and smooth with an icing knife before serving.

Tips and tricks

- *I prefer using the brownie tin if I'm making the cake for smoko. It means that you can cut the cake into good-sized handfuls rather than wedges. If the cake is cooked in a rectangular tin it is also a little faster to cool and ice.*
- *Coconut is a nice addition to the top.*

Summer

Lamb marking

I would normally consider myself an early riser, but setting the alarm for five in the morning is never easy. By late November this is my reality. The sun rises with me, and the robust canvas smoko bags are packed and picked up before five-thirty, when the first truck of shepherds leaves for the first morning muster. We call this time of year lamb marking, also known in other parts of New Zealand as docking and tailing. I think we must have borrowed the term 'lamb marking' from our merino neighbours in Australia where you hear it called this too.

Apparently an early bird catches the worm, and in our case the early shepherd has better luck moving the mobs of merino in the cooler temperatures of the early mornings. It is also the first time the lambs have come into contact with humans and dogs, and they need to take it easy to ensure none are left behind.

Lamb marking takes place when the lambs are about two or three months old. It's a time for us to give the lambs a six-in-one vaccine against diseases

OPPOSITE: A pen of merino lambs.

ABOVE: Lamb marking in the early 1960s. Those pictured include
Ray Cleave, Jim Lousley, Joe Cameron (my husband's grandfather),
Norman Morris and Preston Cameron.

as well as mark them with an ear notch to indicate their sex and origin. Even though the lambs receive ear tags at weaning time (when the lambs are old enough to be separated from their mothers), the notch is permanent and allows us to identify any stock that may lose their tag in scrub or on rocks. Each farm in our area has a distinct ear notch, so it's also a way of identifying stock if they've gone for a wander.

It also helps at other times in the year when sheep are run through the race, and the person drafting them can quickly glance at their sex and flock before separating them into different pens. However, we are looking into new technology around this practice. One option could be to use electronic identification (EID) tags from early on, but there are issues to work through around stock wrangling and the retention of tags in the tough terrain.

During lamb marking, each lamb is picked up out of a pen and sent down a chute to get their treatments. After the lamb's sex is determined, the ram lambs are castrated and are then termed wethers.

The lambs are not the only ones getting attention at this time of year. We also check the health of the ewes. A ewe who was scanned with a lamb but hasn't successfully cared for one, either because she miscarried or the lamb hasn't survived after birth, is called a wet-dry. She will have her EID tag scanned and the information is recorded electronically. If she is unsuccessful at breeding two years in a row, then she is culled from the breeding programme.

The other task we do at lamb marking is shortening the lambs' tails. We use a hot iron to cleanly cut and seal the wound. The tail is removed for a number of reasons — mostly to do with poo — and shortened to a length that protects the lambs' bottoms. If poo attaches to the tail wool, this creates what's known as a dag. Poo attracts flies, the flies lay eggs, and maggots hatch to feast on the poo. They then begin to feast on the lamb's flesh and can slowly eat the lamb alive. This is called fly strike. Removing the tail reduces the

OPPOSITE: (Top left) Flora patting Ike, a favourite station horse.
(Top right) Earning myself a cuppa by lifting lambs. (Below) Me and
Sarah Scott assisting Gandy Burrows as he castrates the ram lambs.

chances of fly strike and significantly increases our lamb survival rate. It's also why farmers regularly crutch their sheep too, meaning they remove any wool and poo from around the sheep's bottoms.

Growing up on a farm, we celebrate life and are honest about what causes death. The girls aren't desensitised, but rather are more aware of it and understand that sometimes animals may become sick or die. They know that we have pet lambs not because they are cute and fuzzy, but because their mothers have died and so it's our duty to care for the lambs. The girls are great little nurturers, although I'm sure it's Joe and I who do most of the feeding. They're in it just for the cuddles.

BECAUSE MERINOS PREFER to be left alone, we don't often have a lot of pet lambs. If we do, it's always at lamb marking time when we can clearly see if a lamb doesn't mother-up again (when a ewe and lamb find each other again after separation). It was just my luck that at my first lamb marking, only a few months after we lost my mother-in-law, I had an unusually large number of nine pet lambs, a blind Hereford bull calf, two children under two to care for, and enormous amounts of food to make each day. I felt like my childhood neighbour Aunty Betty, who used to boast about how many people she had fed for lunch each day and would adopt every orphaned animal under the sun. I made up big buckets of milk that had to be poured into individual bottles, and was out feeding the lambs morning and night. That year Joe built a feeder that allowed me to put several bottles in at once, which made a huge difference. But we haven't used it again, as since then we've had fewer than three pet lambs and one very cute Hereford bull calf named Jackson-Cow.

One year not long after I returned from overseas and moved in with Joe, I got my first pet lamb at Otematata and I called her Pru. She was a spoilt lamb who didn't have to share my affection and attention with anyone else, and by the time she was weaned off the bottle she had developed a taste for silverbeet. Each day I would give her a large helping from my crop in the vege garden. I remember my friend Hamish saying to me once, when it was the only thing he could grow in his Central Otago vege garden, that silverbeet would be the perfect feed to plant for sheep because it grows back so quickly once nibbled down and it winters well. Pru had come from a mob of studs — a flock that we keep to breed desired traits in merinos, such as wool properties and strong bodies for healthy sheep — but with no credentials to trace, she was unable to go back in with the studs. Instead, when she was old enough she was mustered out with a flock of ewe hoggets to their summer spot near the back of the property. Merinos are a lean bunch, and I had loved Pru into a very round, affectionate lamb who got easily out of breath. She was marked with a large orange ear tag to identify her on return, and we said our goodbyes one morning before I left to go and teach. It wasn't long into the muster before Hugh had to put one fat, puffing pet lamb into the back of the truck for the rest of the journey; and either Pru is one of the woollies that has escaped the muster for many years, or perhaps she was put out by the lack of silverbeet on the hills, but she has never made it home again. Maybe this is one of those stories your parents tell you, that 'Your old dog has gone to retire on a friends farm', and Joe and Hugh are yet to tell me the truth.

LAMB MARKING IS A SOCIAL TIME of year. We work outside in the hint of summer — add good food, banter, music and the promise of a cold beer afterwards, and you've a recipe for a great lamb marking. I've worked in a few summer tailing gangs over the years, but none as enjoyable as when I would help Kate and Phil Rive at Cecil Peak Station near Queenstown.

Our friendship began when I was 23, as a chance encounter while boating with friends in Queenstown. I had never been across Lake Wakatipu before and, after perching on a spot on the beach in front of the Cecil Peak woodshed, I was shortly introduced to Kate. Conversation came easily, and soon I was taking every opportunity I could to visit and work for them. The lifestyle, their friendship and the environment were inspiring. I learnt so much from them, including the importance of holding a scrim — a long piece of hessian that creates a barrier — to avoid a lamb-break (when young lambs dart in every direction but the right one) and the unusual fact that sheep can swim.

It's not until now, living with my own family on a large station, that I fully understand how much Kate and Phil influenced me. They are fabulous employers, have a great rapport with their employees and the merino industry, and are a bloody good laugh.

At the time, I was teaching in Clyde and would often squeeze in as much time as I could at Cecil Peak. The station is unreachable by road due to the lake and mountains. I would leave for the lake straight after school on Friday evening and have Phil zip me back early Monday morning before the bell. One particular weekend, the boat had some engine troubles and I had to ring the principal to apologise that I wasn't going to make it back in time. The principal took the opportunity to have a morning back in the classroom, and the children had a fun writing prompt that afternoon when I told them about being landlocked.

I recently listened to Kiwi farming broadcaster Sarah Perriam describe how it's not her net worth but her network that enriches her. She went on to exclaim, 'And I know a hell of a lot of people.' I really identify with this. Over time, it's been my connections with people on the land that have enriched my life.

Chance encounters are also how we came to have some high school students work on the station this summer. When we were living in Christchurch, I went on school camp with my class to Wainui on Banks Peninsula. One of the dads who was helping out told me how he and his wife used to live down the road at the French Farm Winery, which they had owned. I began to tell

OPPOSITE: (Top left) A pen of ewes and their lambs.
(Top right) Sarah drafting the flock. (Below) A team of dogs
watching on as they rest after their morning of mustering.

him that I believed my sister Christy had managed the restaurant there at one point, which instantly sparked an enthusiastic conversation because we discovered she had in fact worked for James and Emily-Jane. Their daughter Franny was in my class, and it was nice to make a new family connection.

Six years later I received an email from Franny, who was in her last year of high school and considering a career in farming. Her words were to the effect of: 'Since my dad won't buy me a farm, I thought I'd come and spend some time with you.' She already had a sense of humour, so I knew she would fit into the tailing gang and be able to give and take a bit of flack. I suggested she bring a friend with her and spend some time with us at lamb marking.

So for a few days, Franny and Tilly came to stay. We were really impressed: they were up at five each morning and quick to learn. Each night they would voluntarily entertain our girls after work, sit with us for dinner, even put the girls to bed and have a bit of banter with us — all before we caught sight of a cellphone. When they returned via helicopter for a shower on their last day before heading home, you could see on their faces that they were hooked on the high country life.

Lamb marking is a great way to introduce young people to the farming industry. It typically coincides with high school and university holidays, making it a great option for casual work. There are always a few old musterers on hand to show the way. One is Gandy Burrows, who has worked in the high country his whole life since beginning at Otematata Station in his mid-twenties. Gandy has returned to our station over the years, in between managing properties and working throughout the South Island. And now in his sixties, Gandy is 'actively retiring' on farm. I like watching Gandy train young shepherds, and they respect his wealth of knowledge. He's known for dishing out nicknames and banter, but he can read a situation and know when to be gentle too. This year, when one of the uni students suggested bringing down their Bluetooth speaker for music, I heard Gandy reply that it was a 'bloody silly idea', only to turn to me and admit that if there was music he wouldn't be able to hear any of the gossip.

Smoko at sunrise

My first experience cooking during lamb marking came about quite randomly one summer when I was at teachers' college. I was gearing up for a summer working in the shearing sheds when Peter Lyon asked if I'd be interested in cooking and nannying for one of his farmers on a high country station. My job was to help care for the three children at home and the two more that would join us once school finished, as well as cook during tailing time. It sounded like an adventure that I shouldn't pass up on, and so I spent that summer working for Kerryn and Dan Thomas at Killermont Station in Lindis Pass.

I was just a novice cook at this stage, and I'm sure they politely ate their way through mediocre smokos and lunches that first summer. My cooking and time management improved as I worked for them over many more summers, and as we bring up our girls I realise too how often I draw on bits of parenting that I learnt from Kerryn. She is one amazing mamma — even just recently when our girls met Kerryn for the first time, they were instantly drawn to her. You can see her mirrored in our own daily routines at home. For example, when Kerryn's children came in from outside at the end of the

ABOVE: A lunch assembly line in the part of the station
we call our 'backyards', 1994.

day, they would enter through the back door and strip off. Clean work clothes were folded up for the next day and the rest dumped into the laundry bin. The kids jumped straight in the shower, and a clean set of clothes would be worn in the evenings. There was no daily afternoon television, and after dinner, which was always around the table where manners were paramount, we were often entertained by impromptu dance-offs and games.

When Joe and I renovated our back door and laundry, I had farm kids in mind. Boots are hung up outside on pegs and the laundry bins pull out for any dirty clothes. There's a shower and toilet just as you walk in, and there's no reason for dirt (or worse) to be walked through the house. Once the girls are in their pyjamas and are waiting for bed we always play games or cards, or read books. It's quality family time, which is especially valuable if Joe hasn't seen the girls all day. Once they've gone to bed, that's when we catch up on the news or anything important.

Despite all my experience cooking on farms over the years, I honestly still find this time of year overwhelming. Each day means a large amount of food, consisting of morning smoko, lunch and enough to cover afternoon smoko for the crew of seven or eight. How I manage to get it all packed by five thirty every morning surprises me. The days are getting hotter by late November, and cooking in the afternoons is not only unappealing but near impossible with the girls at home. Instead we often head to the lake for a swim and a barbecue tea, and I cook later once the girls have gone to bed. By the time I've washed the last pot it's near eleven, and I set the alarm for five to boil the billy in the morning for the thermos.

All the food needs to be able to travel, sit in the smoko bags during the day without spoiling, and be eaten with hands. Typically I'll prepare two savoury smoko items, one large savoury lunch item and two sweet items. I pack them in old cake tins and then into several old canvas Susie bags that have stood

OPPOSITE: (Top) Sarah Scott bravely agreeing to try one of Flora's iced Christmas cookies. (Below) A good time for a yarn and a laugh over smoko.

the test of time and will outlive me, I'm sure. When Mandy passed I inherited her stash of plastic containers, but I've found that over the past two years they've cracked and broken.

This year, Hugh made a good job of finishing them off. One morning after smoko it had started to rain, and Hugh placed the smoko bags under the Land Cruiser to keep them dry. Several mobs later, and a location change had the gang packing up to move on. Hugh jumped into the truck and, forgetting his plan to keep lunch dry, proceeded to run over the bags squashing most of the contents.

I was in town that day and received a guilty-sounding voicemail from Hugh admitting the mistake and suggesting I go and purchase some new containers. I'm not a fan of plastic in the kitchen, and so I popped into a secondhand store and found the most incredible stash of old tin cake tins. Even if they are to suffer the same fate as the plastic ones, I know they could be reshaped or dropped at the scrap-metal dealers in town. According to Sarah, our shepherd, rhubarb cake is just as tasty when a little squashed.

It's not often there are any leftovers at this time of year, and if there are I am always reminded of a story that an old neighbour and good friend of Mandy's told me. As a young shepherd herself, Rachel was given advice from a farmer who said that the best way to compliment the cook is to ensure tins are empty when they're returned to the kitchen. Either the gang is well fed or the team of dogs are — I'd like to think it's not the latter. There are, however, usually a few crumbs left in the tins, and our girls enjoy unzipping the returned smoko bags for a wee snack before dinner while we unpack and wash the mugs and thermoses for the next day.

OPPOSITE: (Top left) The view from the 'middle paddock' yards. (Top right) Sarah Scott, Jarrod Solomon and David Cochrane resting up after lifting lambs all morning. (Below) Enamel cups waiting to be filled.

THE MAJORITY OF LAMB marking happens in five different spots on farm, and the shepherds muster the mobs daily to the yards that are closest. Each has its own breathtaking view, and I can't think of a better spot to sip a strong coffee from an enamel mug. (I always forget to pop a spoon in the bag so everyone ends up shaking in little piles of coffee.) While the kids are of preschool age I want to make the most of these opportunities to drop off smoko together to such fabulous spots. Whether our trips involve a mug of Raro (the girls none the wiser that I have diluted it), helping Grandad with tailing rings on the elastrator, chasing lambs into the pens or stealing a ride on Gandy's gentle-giant horse Wallie, we're creating memories and instilling the girls with a sense of responsibility for the land and animals here at Otematata. I can only imagine that once they're older, going out with Mum at smoko time won't be so cool anymore, and they'll be escaping out the door early with the rest of the workers.

The outdoors on our doorstep

When Joe and I decided to come home to the farm, we did so with our future family in the front of our minds. We wanted to be present in our children's lives, and to provide them with the kind of rural upbringing that we both had. It wasn't an easy decision, with Joe's passion for the airline industry, but when we tuck the girls into bed each night and see those worn-out faces with big smiles, I feel sure we made the right choice.

While teaching in private schools in New Zealand and Australia I saw a lot of children dropped at before-school care early in the morning, only to go into after-school in the afternoon until their parents had finished work. These parents were driven, successful and motivated, with careers in medicine, law, business and other time-demanding professions. They worked hard every day to provide their kids with a great education. However, the more I saw students asleep in their ties and blazers in beanbags at five on a weekday,

OPPOSITE: Aoraki Mount Cook watching over us as Gandy Burrows gets the girls ready for a ride on Wally, his trusty steed.

waiting to be picked up, the more I wondered if both parents working such long hours was worth it.

Being a parent is one of the most selfless vocations. As important as it is to care for yourself and your mental wellbeing, as soon as you have kids everything feels bigger than just yourself. Joe and I are in this parenting gig together, so when we need time to refresh our minds and recharge the batteries, we play tag: Joe will occasionally get in nine holes of golf before lunch on a Saturday, and then I will tag out and hop out on my mountain bike for the afternoon, or pop into our sleep-out to sew. If Joe goes away duck-shooting the first weekend in May, I take a weekend later in the year for a pamper and a shop. I sometimes think in some relationships people forget there are *two* parents — childcare isn't the sole responsibility of the mother, and so I love that Joe and I are on the same page when it comes to parenting.

I'm one of those people who has never felt comfortable leaving the girls with grandparents or family for a weekend away, and I don't know if this is because I became a parent in my thirties — as opposed to my mum's generation, who became parents in their early twenties — but I don't feel I need to be anywhere else. I was social enough in my early twenties to fulfil a lifetime, and then in my mid-twenties I discovered multisport, time-consuming but so rewarding.

So after all that, I don't feel a need to rush. I'm happy working on farm with the girls at home, popping out weekly to kindy or to see other mums, getting out on farm with Joe and the girls, or simply making the most of all the wonderful things we have on our doorstep.

I'VE ALWAYS BEEN DRAWN to hot and dry climates. Before I met Joe I spent a lot of time in Central Otago, where I taught for many years. It was there, after support-crewing for my friend Deb's husband Charlie in the Coast to Coast multisport event, that I got caught up in the buzz and decided I wanted to compete the following year.

It all began with a ten-kilometre run in Alexandra, then a half-marathon in Dunedin, and eventually I was purchasing a two-day individual Coast to Coast entry that saw me run, cycle and kayak 243 kilometres from the west coast of the South Island to the east. I was hooked, and knew I would be back to do it the next year. In between I threw myself into other adventure sport events, like the Goldrush three-day multisport event (as a team) that circled its way around historic gold-mining spots in Central Otago, the Gutbuster endurance mountain bike race through Nevis Valley, the iconic Motatapu mountain bike race from Wanaka to Arrowtown, and lots of small ones that helped prepare me for the bigger races.

It was a privilege and thrill to take part in these, with a common theme of dry, dusty tracks, summits more than a thousand metres above sea level, and access to tracks through some of the most beautiful hillsides covered in strong scented wild thyme.

Little did I know when I began, adventure sport was exactly what I needed to take stock of my life and motivate me to make goals for the future. I thrived on the weekly routine of training, which I did before and after school, and on the weekends. And I felt motivated to try new things, meet new people and go on adventures I would never have imagined.

When I entered the Coast to Coast for the first time, I didn't know where to begin. I owned a mountain bike and a pair of running shoes, which would get me so far, but I lacked one major essential skill — the ability to kayak the 67-kilometre stretch of the Waimakariri River, known for its white water rapids that run from the bottom of the Southern Alps through mountain gorges towards the east coast of the South Island. So I rang the local guru of adventure racing and multisport in Central Otago, Bill Godsall, and asked if he knew any coaches who would be willing to take on a newbie like me. Thankfully he took me under his wing himself, and became a dear friend. We spent hours each week either in the kayaks or on our bikes covering an incredible number of kilometres together, debating all sorts of topics, from travel and New Year's resolutions to relationship advice and gossip. If I wasn't out training with Bill or friends, I was out on my own, following my feet and in my head making goals.

I must admit that multisport is an incredibly selfish hobby — I can't imagine fitting it into family life and being able to justify the cost of entries, new equipment and time away from home. When training I would make the most of daylight hours after school, and then duck back after tea to prepare for the next day's lessons.

The friendships and memories that I made will last a lifetime, but above all I gained a belief in myself and what I could achieve, and this is what wrote the next chapter of my life. I think a lot about my last trip down the Waimakariri River. One section was particularly crowded, and several of us went into a rapid together where I capsized and clung onto my boat until I was retrieved by a jet boat. Unfortunately the person in the jet boat let go of my kayak as I was climbing on board and, long story short, by the time I saw it again it was quite battered. One roll of duct tape later and I was on my way down the river again. Despite having no experience in a longboat kayak before entering the Coast to Coast, the river was my favourite section and I became a strong paddler. The same solitary hours that I spent in my head nutting out future goals were also good for bringing up self-doubt, and after I'd stopped and emptied my waterlogged boat several times I was starting to feel lost. I'd hoped to improve a lot on my initial Coast to Coast time, but that was near impossible now with my boat being split nearly in two down the seams. As I reached the stretch of water at Woodstock, I felt defeated and was about to pull out of the race. The tape was failing and it was taking too much energy to paddle myself and a boat full of water. At a smooth stretch, I pulled up on a beach where a group of women in red hats were having an elaborate picnic and cheering on the competitors.

I later found out that these ladies were a part of the Red Hat Society — an international group dedicated to reshaping the way women are viewed in

OPPOSITE: Preparing the smoko bag
for a day on the hill.

today's culture. The red-hatters support and encourage women to pursue fun, friendship, freedom, and fulfilment of lifelong dreams and fitness.

I can't quite remember the entire interaction, but quitting was not in these ladies' vocabularies. As one red-hatter and I emptied my boat of half the river, a competitor in a sea kayak (which nearly made me cry — because if the sea kayaks had caught up then I had really lost a lot of time) threw a roll of duct tape at the beach. I was so grateful, as I had none left. The red-hatter looked at me and said, 'You might not be as screwed as you thought — we've got this,' and as one held the bow and another the stern, they rotated the boat while I duct-taped around and around and around. And I finished the race. I made it to Sumner Beach before the one-day competitors caught up, and in a similar time than my previous year. (I could only dream of what my time would be if I hadn't lost my boat!)

What an incredible group of women who, in one small interaction, empowered me not just to finish but also to become an active member in our community today.

We are so fortunate to have nature's playground in our backyard. Not far from the farm gate are Lake Benmore to the north and Lake Aviemore to the east. Constructed in the sixties, Lake Benmore is New Zealand's largest manmade lake and sits behind a remarkable amount of earth and engineering. The dam straddles the valley and embraces the cool water, which changes colour from emerald green to glacial blue with the weather's mood. Lake Aviemore flows from the bottom of Benmore Dam down Waitaki Valley, snaking past the Camerons' original Aviemore homestead.

Joe is a natural sportsperson, and so it is no surprise that he is a great waterskier. When we first met, Joe and our friend Craig taught me to waterski, and this is when I realised how patient and calm Joe is. They spent a good hour that day teaching me to get up on two skis (the only person frustrated was me), and the next year I learnt how to drop a ski and single-ski. I've

OPPOSITE: The garden looking green and bright
before the dry of the summer.

already decided that when the girls are teenagers, Joe will be the one to teach them how to drive.

That first summer we met, Joe also taught me how to reverse a boat trailer. We all have mental checklists of desired attributes in our potential partners, and obviously on Joe's was the ability to back a boat trailer down a loading ramp. Joe set up two drums in the paddock outside his parents' house and we spent an afternoon practising. When it was clear that we were practised out, we made our way up to the big house as I vented my frustrations. I was mortified to find Joe's grandma Mary had arrived and was sitting in the armchair near the front door, reading. I couldn't believe that her first impression of me would involve Joe and I arguing over my stubborn pride! I was relieved to find out that Mary was quite deaf, and wouldn't have heard a word.

Each time I reverse the six-metre boat trailer down the ramp or up the bank at the small Lake Benmore parking area, I always feel a rush of pride. It doesn't mean I don't get nervous, though. Whenever there's a queue I get this feeling that everyone is watching and critiquing me. It doesn't help that our trailer has an annoying American braking system that requires a pin to be placed in the trailer before reversing — this means turning the tight circle leading to the ramp and jumping out to pop in the pin. It's usually at this moment when people get impatient if there's a line. The extra 30 seconds it takes obviously feels like a lifetime to them. Worrying about wasted time is wasted time, in my opinion.

The summers here are dry and hot with temperatures in the thirties, and the autumns are clear, crisp and calm — perfect weather and conditions for boating with friends and family. We spend a lot of time either at the lakes with the boat, or down at Loch Laird at the base of Benmore Dam, swimming and having barbecues. On the afternoons when the heat is too much to bear I will pack up a salad, sausages and chops, and even put a few new potatoes in the magic pot so that we can have them hot with tea on the lake's edge. My

OPPOSITE: My grandma Vyna helping butter the bread for
Evelyn's birthday party at Loch Laird.

magic pot is what I call my multicooker, which never ceases to amaze me with its kitchen wizardry.

The picnic blanket and chairs never leave the canopy of our truck, and the wetsuits and life jackets are on full rotation between there and the washing line. Often I'll pack up the kids and the dog, then give Joe a call to let him know where we'll be so he can meet us there after work. The girls swim and play until we eat, and then once we've packed up it's home for a quick shower, or straight into their pyjamas and bed. The girls' bedrooms face south, and in the summer it's near impossible to keep them cool. We put up a sail outside their rooms to block some of the heat, but the better strategy that we employ on hot nights is to tucker them out so they fall asleep with sheer exhaustion.

Recently we bought a new ski boat, retiring the old farm jet boat (or returning it, depending on which Cameron you speak to). It was an easy decision to make when we live where we do, but it was also an investment into our family life. I have this theory that if we empower the girls with as many skills as we can, then they won't get bored when they're teenagers. If they want to bring friends home for the weekend and spend it on the water trying out new tricks, or simply laughing and enjoying themselves, then that's better than them finding their rush elsewhere. I'll have to work on my cool parent persona so they actually want to bring their friends home in the first place.

January and the first week in February are filled with birthdays and anniversaries, so by default we find ourselves at the lake with friends and family to celebrate. The loch is ideal for children because we can keep an eye on them from the beach and it gradually increases in depth. In fact we have been concealing the fact that there's a pool at the farm homestead from the children for the past five years because its depth intimidates me. We love inviting our friends and their children up from Kurow, which often gets a cold blast from the coast in the afternoons, to our wee slice of paradise.

OPPOSITE: (Top left) Flora having fun with her friends' inflatable toys.
(Top right) 'Sheepy', the cake Evelyn requested for her birthday.
(Below) Friends and their kids enjoying the late afternoon at the lake.

We live more than 25 kilometres from our closest friends, and 70 from our furthest who we see regularly. It's not uncommon to see parents dressing children in pyjamas when we leave a barbecue or party, so that by the time they get home they can simply transfer any sleeping children into their beds. Distance is never a thought in your mind when you crave social interaction.

We celebrated Evelyn's third birthday in 2020 at our usual spot at the lake. There were no bouncy castles, themed tables or grazing platters — we just upsized our usual evening routine. The calm weather and good company were all we needed to make it a success. Everyone swam, the older children took the younger ones for rides on the paddleboard, the dads got to enjoy a mid-week catch-up off farm (which mums get to do on a kindy day), and of course there was a cake.

I love making the girls' birthday cakes. I remember sleepovers at my friend Anna's house near Herbert Forest where we spent hours poring over the *Australian Women's Weekly Children's Birthday Cake Book* and choosing our next cake. Our birthdays could have been nine months away but we thought it good to be prepared. I don't own that particular book now, but we do have *The Great New Zealand Birthday Cake Book*, and the girls have already planned their cakes for the next three years. This time Evelyn went off-script and commissioned a 'Sheepy' cake. Sheepy is her beloved toy sheep that she goes to bed with each night, so well-loved that the fluff has rubbed off its tail.

ON FARM WE HAVE several huts that are used throughout the year for hunters and musterers. One that we love to stay in ourselves is Forks Hut, which sits near the fork of the Clearstream and the Otematata River. There are a collection of huts here that show the progression of years, from locally sourced stone held in place with clay from the banks of the river, to more modern ones made from corrugated iron. The newest hut, built in 2010, is spacious and is used to cook and entertain. It replaced an old Otematata Village 'T house',

which is what most huts on our property are — relocated remnants of the workers' village from the Benmore Dam project in the sixties. Next to the main hut is a bunk house that sleeps ten. All the huts are still used and are popular spots for fishermen and hunters.

Before the huts is a small bridge that crosses the Clearstream. I love this bridge. It's always in full sunlight and is made from smooth planks of wood, so after a swim in the current that flows underneath, you can jump onto the soft boards to warm up. Joe brought me out here the summer we first met, and I was instantly hooked on the magic of the property. There is seldom the wind that can spoil a day on the lake, and there is no noise. It is silent except the sound of the river and the occasional bird.

Now when we take the girls out in summer we rebuild the dam of stones that falls down each year with the movement of the river, and make a wee pool for the girls to play in near the bridge. Going down to the river to fill up the metal bucket for tea and Milos may seem novel. But for the girls it's creating memories, and for Joe and me it's a chance to teach the girls about sourcing clean water and being careful near the river's edge.

ABOVE: Forks Hut, pictured in 1952.

We like to bring friends out to Forks Hut too. This last New Year's we invited our friends Jane and Ray and their three children to this spot and spent the day doing . . . well, not much. We ate, shared some drinks and watched the kids play in the river. Our girls had got new fishing rods for Christmas, and the novelty of lowering the sinker over the edge of the bridge was nearly as great as the idea that they might catch something. (Of course we would never truly fish this way in the Clearstream, which is a well coveted catch-and-release fly-fishing spot for regulars who book years in advance.)

Joe and I feel it's important for our girls to become confident swimmers, not only with our immediate environment in mind but because New Zealand is essentially made up of islands. Every school term from when the girls were nine months old, I've organised my weekly day in town around their swimming lessons. With the help of my mum (known to the girls as Nanny), who lives in town, we cram a lot into a day in Oamaru.

Nanny meets us at the library in the morning, where the girls fill their bags with books, and while they're busy I get 40 minutes to cram in all the farm errands. This time alone is precious — ordinarily I'm limited by how long it takes to unclick the girls' car seats, get them out, try and stop them from wanting to touch and see every single object in a place even if it's a plumbing store, and then get them back into the car seats, only to repeat this at the next store. It really does suck the soul dry some days, so when Nanny minds them at the library I may also make the most and squeeze in a treat takeaway coffee. It always amuses me when Joe makes a comment about my 'town day', as if I'm getting my hair and nails done. By the time I drive around trying to find the correct bolts or pipe fitting, take the girls to all their activities and get the groceries, the day is almost over.

During the working week we always sit at the table for mealtimes. I can't remember the last time we watched the news at six or ate dinner on our knees. Instead, we feel it's important to make family time paramount, discussing our days and encouraging the girls to be open. Since we lost Mandy, my father-in-law comes for tea once a week too. It's not so much for the food,

as Hugh is a great cook himself and even enjoys preserving produce from his extensive vegetable garden, but the girls love the sense of occasion. Grandad will encourage the nibbling of mutton fat from the roast or the drowning of pudding in cream. If it's summer then he'll join us at the lake for a sausage too, and in the cooler months he'll leave after tucking the girls into bed with a few stories. It doesn't matter what the day's held, if the food is enjoyed and everyone is exhausted, then it's been a success.

Weaning

Towards the end of January, as the holidaymakers head back to work and vacate the lakes, their camping spots and holiday homes, the cold easterly that always interrupts a good day on the lake dies down, and the weather settles.

It doesn't mean that we can stop and bask in the sun, but we do get up early to avoid the heat, work, and then enjoy the afternoons. Daylight savings still sees days stretch into the night, especially this far down the South Island. At this time of year we begin to wean the lambs from the ewes. At four months old the lambs are now able to digest vegetable matter, and weaning

ABOVE: Pup Houston (seated) supervising lunch, 1994.

gives the ewe a chance to put on some condition after feeding her lamb for so long. It's similar to when a baby begins to eat solids, and the mum's body gets a break from being their only food source.

Over the next month we will wean three distinct flocks separated for management of large numbers: our Aviemore, Otematata and stud flocks. Each flock is mustered separately and brought down from its lambing country to the closest set of yards. Even though some days I can drive out and deliver the food to the yards, most of the time the smoko bags leave at five-thirty in the morning with the musterers. Like always, the shepherds should be able to eat the food with their hands, but it's also important at this time of year for the food to last in the heat without spoiling. Cold chicken drumsticks sitting in the smoko bag with temperatures in the high twenties? No thank you.

Overall we will wean 10,000 lambs, which will either replace our older ewes and wethers or be sold as store lambs. Any surplus lambs are sold to other farms to bolster their numbers. The ewes are returned to their summer country on the hills, and the lambs are placed on the protein-rich crops grown here on our newly developed and irrigated flats. Joe will have worked with our seed technician and agronomist, a specialist in soil management and crop development, to make sure the right amount of food has grown to support the lambs through the winter months until we shear. After shearing they will join their flock of origin.

At our other property near Kurow we breed a Suffolk and merino lamb for its meat value. It is sold through Silere, who are dedicated to providing the best-quality grass-fed merino meat to the world. To sell to them we must follow strict guidelines to make sure the consumer is only getting the best quality. For example, even though our sheep are at home in paddocks of green grass, we are unable to bolster their feed with grain because the worldwide perception of grain-fed sheep is one of cramped feedlots — so best quality means ensuring our sheep consume only grass. When the Silere team call

OPPOSITE: Heading home after dropping off smoko.

in for a cuppa and talk through our accreditation, it's easy to reflect on our stewardship of the land and animals. It's exciting to play a part in a product that's so proud of what it offers the world.

New Zealand is world-leading in its farming approaches. I believe we need to be benchmarking against other countries, instead of only each other, to showcase our strengths. The individual goals we set ourselves on farm are based on benchmarking statistics within our own country. Let's take a moment and see where we sit in the world because, despite new legislation being thrown at us from our own government, we constantly rise to the challenge and excel. Let's celebrate our grass-fed, antibiotic-free, hill-roaming free-range stock. As farmers are often a humble bunch and our voices are quiet, now is a chance to share our positive farming practices with the world. Local and global companies are demanding sustainable fibres and food from farms that care for their land and soil health, and which encompass the five freedoms of animal welfare. We can not only provide this, we can pave the way.

As the thousands of lambs and ewes are run through the yards for weaning, it's also another chance to check their health and administer any preventatives they may need, such as drench to deal to any worms, and dip to exterminate external parasites that can cause discomfort to the sheep. The word 'dip' is derived from an old method in which the sheep took an actual dip in a narrow pool, but now it's far more technological and accurate. The sheep run through a race where a laser administers a calculated amount of 'dip' to their tops, bottoms and sides. It is far more efficient, safer for the farmers' health, cost-effective and less stressful to the animals. The lambs are also given another six-in-one vaccine, the same as what they received at lamb-marking, which boosts their immunity.

OPPOSITE: A shot taken from the helicopter
of cattle heading over the hills.

AN ENORMOUS VOLUME OF food is cooked and demolished over the weeks of weaning, with a staff of seven or eight. We are always grateful to have Lincoln University students on staff at this time of year for help with weaning, and, with many of them studying agriculture, they are usually after some course credits. There is something surreal about witnessing the amount of food young university students can put away. It's like they're filling up before another year of flatting, when their budget for groceries is prioritised between socialising and course costs.

The first weaning that I cooked on my own, I soon learnt that it took a large toll on me and our young family. While I like to cook either early in the morning before the girls get up or after they've gone to bed, I was soon resembling a candle with a wick burning at both ends. It was then that we discussed hiring some help one day a week while I went to town for groceries and the girls' swimming lessons, meaning I wouldn't have to cook late into the night after returning from the 200-kilometre round trip.

And so Vicky, our Wednesday wonder woman, entered our lives. Vicky lives in the Otematata township, and had previously helped with housework after my C-section with Evelyn. To be honest she never stopped coming — we just asked her to join our staff one day a week. Vicky enjoys the quiet of the empty house and knows my pantry layout better than I do. I've been known to message her when trying to find a utensil or an ingredient, and even with my vague descriptions she always knows exactly what I'm looking for and puts me right.

Each week I'll leave a menu for Vicky to whip up. There is no better feeling than walking into the house after a long day away knowing that the food for the next day is covered. All I have to do the next morning is fill the thermoses and smoko bags before the pick-up time. There isn't much that Vicky doesn't do for us except feed my chickens — there's sometimes a rat situation in the coop and she isn't fond of the scurrying wee buggers.

OPPOSITE: (Top) Evelyn and Flora hunting for strawberries.
(Below) Flora enjoys the vege garden as much as I do.

Vicky makes this one recipe that I can never master like she does. It's a chocolate-chip biscuit by Chelsea Winter, and Vicky's are always round, soft and delicious. Mine? Little rocks that crumble. However there is one American-style cookie recipe I've mastered which Vicky can't, by Anna Cameron (a Kiwi food blogger known as Just a Mum). Where one of us fails, the other excels. Vicky and I are quite a pair in the kitchen.

Jars, shows and sales

Just as I think I'm busy enough with all the cooking and the children, the fruit on the trees ripens. I love preserving fruit. There is something special about the occasion of it, and Mandy used to sum it up perfectly. She called it 'squirrelling', foraging all the fruit and vegetables and preserving them for the year ahead. I like this notion. There is nothing more rewarding than reaching up high for a jar of homemade chutney, or fruit to go on the family's cereal.

Here at our cottage we have two apricot trees, a very sad-looking peach tree and an indecisive plum that is never sure if it wants to fruit. I usually have a good crop of tomatoes and potatoes, and any other vegetable that the birds, white butterflies and rabbits haven't managed to consume. I've also secured picking rights at a few holiday homes in the village, which helps me squirrel away even more jars of preserves. Over the years I have learnt a lot about preserving through trial and error, and by going through old recipe books. The use of mace, cloves and large amounts of malt vinegar in most chutneys and sauces can make everything taste the same, and so I've come to scale back the spices and let the flavour of the fruit be more prominent.

This year I found an old Agee preserver in the cellar at the homestead. It's a large 30-litre stainless-steel pot with an element inside, which I fill with a bucket and can easily empty with the tap at the front. I remember Mandy pulled it out of a shed when she tried her hand at making cheese a few years ago. This has made processing jars of fruit so much easier, allowing me to

OPPOSITE: Making Spicy Apricot Sauce (see page 146). I'm funnelling the sauce into empty Barker's bottles, which are great for repurposing.

prepare larger batches. But where there's ease, there's also difficulty. The old element has a knack for overloading the circuit board, and we would be in a dangerous predicament if one of the girls turned on the tap and boiling water burst out. Now I find myself prepping and processing fruit into the night when there are no unnecessary appliances on, and the girls are safe in bed. When I do finally make it to bed, I am lulled to sleep listening to the distinctive pops of a successful seal.

My mum and grandma are also seasoned preservers. Just as we wean lambs and calves at this time of year, I've had to wean myself off stealing jars from my mum. As a child all our preserves were stored inside an old pantry in a little hut outside the house, opposite the kitchen window. I remember one year when Mum had surplus tomatoes and made lots of homemade spaghetti, she asked my eldest sister Hannah to go and get a couple of jars for tea. Out drudged Hannah (her being seven years older than me, my memories of her are mostly as a sassy teenager), who came back alarmed that the spaghetti was 'glowing in the dark'. The spaghetti pasta in the jars of rich red sauce was so white it was almost illuminated, and that year Mum couldn't get us to eat any of it at all.

AS THE SHEEP WEANING wraps up, the girls and I begin to make entries for the Wanaka A&P Show Home Industry Exhibit. The show is held in early March and is always a highlight in the calendar. The weather is spectacular without fail, and it's a great chance to see friends from other rural areas. Held over two days, the show pretty much consumes the town of Wanaka. Every year the showgrounds are extended to accommodate the new stalls and displays.

Each year in February I download the Home Industry catalogue and we choose what to enter. Flora and Evelyn have both been successful the past two years, bringing home ribbons and prize money. I use Pinterest to find inspiration for the girls' entries, but make sure that they are in total control, so much so that once, when Evelyn was two, she burned her finger from hot-gluing a googly eye to a fish in her underwater-themed egg carton creation. It sounds a little intense for a two-year-old, but I desperately wanted her entry to be authentic. Things have been scaled back a bit since then.

Wanaka is an hour and half away, and to make the most of the show we set aside the whole long weekend. Joe prefers we browse the stalls without him, so he often joins us on the final day for rides and candyfloss.

On the morning of the first day, walking into the shed that houses decorated pinecones, vegetable characters and finger-paintings is thrilling. Flora and Evelyn run off to find their creations and see if they've won a prize. Not only do they receive a little bit of pocket money and certificates, but they get ribbons which will hang pride of place in their bedrooms. Throughout the year they often chatter about what to make next, and what they could win.

I've tried a few entries myself over the past few years, without much success. The first year I entered some preserves and jams only to find there's strict protocol around how full jars should be, and how they should be presented. It is quite a serious affair!

The sideshows are just as I remember them from when I was a kid. There's the smell of popcorn and candyfloss in the air, red cheeks no matter how much sunblock you apply, and money kept aside for rides disappears in a flash. Although, I had forgotten how nauseating a merry go round or Ferris wheel is, and the toddler-sized gaps on the rides are enough to put any mother on the edge of an anxiety attack.

AS WE NEAR APRIL we begin to think about weaning the cattle in time for the Omarama Calf Sale. In 2020 we weaned 323 calves across both properties, Otematata Station and Little Awakino near Kurow. We keep the heifers (a cow that has not borne a calf) for replacements, and sell on any Hereford steers (castrated males) and all of the Angus and Hereford crosses.

If the stars align we might wean the Little Awakino calves on a Tuesday, meaning I can drop off the smoko and lunch on my way past the yards to the Hakataramea kindy with the girls. Rather than having to get up early to prepare the smoko bags, I can work at a more respectable hour and not worry about the shepherds dropping by while I'm still in my dressing gown.

The Omarama Calf Sale has become a family outing. We sit in the stands and watch as each lot is bid on and sold. It's organised chaos as calves are rotated through the viewing pen at the front of the stand. The auctioneer's voice rings out above the sound of the cattle and the calls from the agents on behalf of potential buyers. There is something exhilarating about an auction — and terrifying your children with the idea that if they move an inch or sneeze they might end up making a bid (it's one way to keep little bottoms in seats for the duration of the sale). The sale is also a chance to show the girls where some of our revenue comes from. Our calves usually do very well in price, and if we're lucky Grandad or Dad will shout us lunch at the Wrinkly Rams on the way home in celebration.

OPPOSITE: Jackson-Cow, named by the girls when he was a very cute pet calf. He still enjoys a Weet-Bix even though he is now weaned and back with his peers.

FOLLOWING: Looking over Loch Laird to the skyline beyond the farm.

Zucchini and Bacon Slice

Makes 1 pie (6–8 slices)

3 eggs, whisked

2 zucchini, grated

1 cup grated cheese

½ onion, grated
(optional)

2 rashers bacon,
chopped

½ cup self-raising flour

¼ cup milk

salt and pepper

This is a tasty way to use up the summertime glut of zucchini, but also a great lunch idea. It can be served warm or cold, so it suits a meal at home, a packed lunch or a picnic at the lake on the weekend.

Preheat the oven to 180°C (350°F) fan-bake. Grease or line a ceramic quiche dish.

In a large bowl, whisk the eggs together. Add the zucchini, cheese, onion (if using) and bacon. Fold through the flour and milk and season to taste with salt and pepper.

Pour the mixture into the prepared dish and bake for 35 minutes.

Tips and tricks

- *This recipe is easily doubled for a big crowd.*
- *If you don't have zucchini, use chopped leeks or kale (sweat them first in a little butter) or silverbeet.*
- *During summer, grate any excess zucchini into a clean tea towel and squeeze out the excess moisture. Pack as much zucchini as you can into silicone moulds and place in the freezer to set. Once frozen, pop the rounds out and store them in an old bread bag or container in the freezer, for use throughout the year.*
- *For a dairy-free option, replace the milk with oil.*
- *If you want to eat this cold from the dish then I'd recommend not using baking paper, as it will sweat. Instead grease the dish well and it will come out perfectly.*
- *If this is going in a packed lunch, turn the slice out and let it cool on a wire rack. Slice once cool, then place in the fridge until needed.*

Picnic Pie

400 g (14 oz) block puff pastry

12 eggs

salt and pepper

500 g (1 lb 2 oz) sausage meat

egg wash or a little milk (optional)

Optional additions

leftover cold new potatoes, or parboiled potatoes cut into chunks

tomatoes

spinach

silverbeet

grated zucchini

spring onions

tomato relish

cheese

This is very similar to the bacon and egg pie, but it's a great way to use up any sausages or sausage meat you may have lingering in your freezer. The sausage meat adds a different texture and is quite filling.

Preheat the oven to 180°C (350°F) fan bake. Set aside a 32 cm x 25 cm (12¾ in x 10 in) pie dish.

Use a knife to mark thirds in the pastry block. Roll two-thirds of the pastry out and use it to line your pie dish, making sure the pastry goes up the edges. Trim any excess away. Roll the final one-third out and cut into long strips to be used as a lattice to top the pie with later.

Break the eggs into your dish and use a clean hand to break the yolks up. (I use my hand so that I don't accidentally pierce the pastry with my fork.) Alternatively, if you prefer your yolks whole, leave them alone. Season with salt and pepper.

Squeeze the sausage meat in little dollops throughout the pie and add any optional extras. Use the strips of pastry to criss-cross your pie to create a lattice. Trim any excess away from the sides. Brush the pastry with egg wash or a little milk if you want a golden top.

Bake for 20–25 minutes.

Tips and tricks

- *You can use as many eggs as you like; a dozen is just a nice round number that I like to use. It won't make much of a difference if you use 10 or 12 or 14.*
- *If you don't have sausage meat, use sausages and squeeze the meat out of the casings.*
- *The lattice strips don't have to be the same size; it looks nice and rustic when they are different sizes.*

Preserving fruit and sauces

I am still learning so much about preserving fruit and vegetables, and every year I become more proficient at it. Over the years I have experimented with so many methods for preserving, while trying to simplify the process, but I keep coming back to the tried, true and tested methods outlined in the *Ball Complete Book of Home Preserving*. I would recommend getting this book to refer to as your home preserving bible.

Jars and bottles

I have a mixture of new and old jars. I like to reuse glass cordial bottles for when I preserve sauces. I find the lids are very reliable for resealing.

I have a collection of Agee jars from my mum and mother-in-law, as well as new Ball jars. You have to find what works well for you.

If you have older jars, make sure you have the correct bands for screwing the seals down. It would be very disappointing if none of your jars sealed.

I keep most of my jam jars to reuse for more jam and chutneys. Be careful not to damage the lids when you open them by tapping a knife around the side or perhaps using a door jamb for opening tricky jars. This will ruin the seal and you won't be able to use them again. Instead invest in a good jar-opener.

Sterilising bottles and jars

Prepare bottles by washing them with a bottle brush in hot, soapy water, rinse well and drain.

Place them in a 120°C (235°F) oven (lie them on the oven racks) for 10–15 minutes.

To sterilise lids, pour boiling water over them and leave them in the water until you need them.

Hot water baths

Hot water baths are used after filling jars to ensure the contents won't spoil on the pantry shelf. There are plenty of options to investigate.

If you are only making small batches of preserves then a small preserving rack that lowers into your jam pan would be a good place to start.

I recently found an electric Agee canner in the homestead cellar that fits a large amount of jars at a time. This makes light work of a big job.

Preserving starter kits are available to buy with a large canning pot and a rack that lowers into the water.

Utensils essential to preserving

- good-quality jam pan or similar canning pot (20 litres; 700 fl oz)
- canning rack
- good-quality glass jars and bottles
- bands that fit your jars
- new seals (you cannot reuse seals)
- jar funnel
- jar lifters
- a little porcelain jug (a plastic one will discolour and taint)

Stewed Fruit

Makes about 3–4 cups, depending on your chosen fruit

1 kg (2 lb 4 oz) clean fruit

¼ cup water

¼ cup sugar

When you are preserving fruit there comes a moment when you simply have had enough of packing jars and making sugary syrups. Instead, stew the remaining fruit and use it in puddings or as a topping on your breakfast cereal. You can also use stewed fruit to make Fruit Leather (see page 134) or Vyna's Golden Fruit Sponge (see page 138).

Wash your fruit and cut up into chunks. Remove any blemishes as well as any stones or pips.

Place in a heavy-bottomed pot with the water and sugar and simmer on a low heat, stirring often. You may need more sugar depending on the fruit you are using. Just taste and add as you need.

When the stewed fruit reaches the consistency that you desire, take it off the heat.

Tips and tricks

- *This is the perfect way to use up any 'ugly' fruit or fruit that has begun to spoil.*
- *You could use honey instead of sugar to sweeten the fruit.*
- *Using a heavy-bottomed pot helps to prevent the fruit from sticking.*
- *Store the stewed fruit in jars (see preserving notes on page 130), or simply freeze it.*
- *Make sure you clearly label your stewed fruit in the freezer. Pumpkin soup and stewed apricots have a similar colour and texture, but only one of them tastes good on your porridge.*

Fruit Leather

Makes about 30 rolls

1 kg (2 lb 4 oz) fruit (stone fruit or berries work best)

2 tablespoons honey

250 g (9 oz) 'hidden' vegetables (see tips and tricks)

There is more madness than method with this recipe. I have given some approximate quantities, but I tend to use stashes of fruit from the freezer or the leftover fruit that doesn't get preserved, so I don't often make it to measure.

Try making the small batch below — as you get more confident you will develop an eye for how you want the pulp to look, and you can adjust the quantities to suit how much fruit you have. The leather takes up to 12 hours to dry, so it is best to make it and leave it to dry overnight.

This recipe also provides a great opportunity to sneak some vegetables into the kids.

Preheat the oven to 60°C (140°F) fan-bake. Line 3–4 oven trays with baking paper.

Stew the fruit and vegetables using the stewed fruit method (see page 132; omit the sugar and just use honey).

Once stewed, use a stick blender to make a smooth pulp.

Spoon 2 or 3 ladles of pulp onto each prepared baking tray, and use an icing knife to smooth it out to a thickness of 2–3 mm (1/16–1/8 in).

Place the trays into the oven and leave overnight.

When you are confident the leather is dry all over, take it out of the oven and allow it to cool.

Leave the leather on the baking paper, cut it into strips and roll up. Use a piece of tape to secure the roll.

Store in an airtight container.

Tips and tricks

- *When hiding veges I like to use ones that have a similar colour to the fruit and are naturally sweet:*
  - *Apricots and carrots or pumpkin*
  - *Green or yellow plums and peas*
  - *Black Boy peaches and peas*
  - *Strawberries and marrow*
- *If you have a marrow appear in the zucchini patch, peel it and take the seeds out. The flesh is white and is easy to hide.*
- *Any excess pulp can be placed in the fridge for you to make a batch the next night.*
- *If you don't have a stick blender, a food processor will work just as well.*
- *I like to store my leather in a jar with a screw lid. It looks pretty on the shelf.*

Vyna's Golden Fruit Sponge

Makes about 6 serves

3 cups stewed fruit

3 eggs

½ cup sugar

¼ cup golden syrup

1 teaspoon vanilla essence

6 tablespoons self-raising flour

3 tablespoons brown sugar

Vyna is my grandma, and I remember this pudding being served after lunch at my grandparents' place most weekends. They always had their main meal at lunchtime and it was always followed by a pud, then Grandad would follow that up with bread, butter and jam. Now we have this pudding most weeks when the girls' grandfather comes for tea. There's something quite special about seeing the girls and their grandad making these memories, bonding over their love of puddings and cream.

This fruit sponge is light and fluffy with hints of caramel. Serve it with cream, ice cream or both.

Preheat the oven to 180°C (350°F) fan-bake.

Place the stewed fruit in a pot or an ovenproof dish (see tips and tricks) and warm gently over a low heat.

Beat the eggs together until light and fluffy. Add the sugar, golden syrup and vanilla essence and beat everything together until the mixture turns pale in colour and is full of body. Fold in the flour.

Once the fruit is hot, transfer it to an ovenproof dish (or use the one you warmed it in). Sprinkle with the brown sugar and pour the sponge batter over the top.

Bake for 35 minutes until the sponge is golden, soft and spongy to the touch.

Tips and tricks

- *It doesn't matter what type of dish you bake the sponge in as long as it is ovenproof. Enamel, ceramic or ovenproof glass are all suitable. I often choose a cast-iron dish that can be used to heat the fruit on the stovetop, so I save on washing up.*

- *Pick your dish size depending on how thick or thin you want your sponge topping. I usually go with a 25–30 cm (10–12 in) dish.*

- *In the middle of winter there's nothing better than a little taste of the summer. Stew and freeze summer fruit for making this pudding.*

- *Tinned fruit works just as well. Black Doris plums, pears and peaches are favourites in our house.*

- *Add ¼ cup of cocoa to the dry ingredients to make a chocolate topping, which pairs nicely with dark fruit.*

Mary's Rich Red Plum Sauce

Makes 4–5 litres

3 kg (6 lb 12 oz) red-fleshed plums

1 onion

1 bulb garlic

1 kg (2 lb 4 oz) sugar

1.5 litres (52 fl oz) malt vinegar

4 teaspoons salt

1 teaspoon cayenne pepper

1 teaspoon ground cloves

2 teaspoons ground ginger

2 teaspoons ground black pepper

I am the third Mrs Cameron to make this plum sauce here at Otematata Station. Seeing we have this wonderful tradition you would think that one of us might have planted a good variety of plums here at the station, but that hasn't happened so far. Not to worry, as I have now sourced a few trees in the village that I am allowed to raid. (Payment currency is, of course, a bottle of sauce.)

Slice the plums in half and remove the stones. Roughly chop the onion and peel the garlic.

Combine all of the ingredients together in a large pot or jam pan and bring to the boil.

Once the mixture has reached a boil, lower the heat and allow the pulp mixture to reduce, stirring often so it doesn't stick to the bottom of the pot or pan. Once reduced, use a stick blender to make a smooth sauce.

Bottle the sauce while it is hot, using a funnel to pour it into hot, sterile bottles, and taking care not to burn yourself. Use a clean cloth to clean the rims before placing the lids on the bottles.

Leave the bottles to seal overnight. There is nothing more satisfying than hearing the lids go 'pop', signifying that they have sealed. Once the bottles have cooled and sealed, wash them in hot, soapy water to get rid of any sticky spots.

»

Tips and tricks

- *During summer I freeze batches of fruit in 3 kg (6 lb 12 oz) bags, so that I can make sauce throughout the year.*

- *I freeze the plums whole, as once they have thawed it's easy to remove the stones by simply squishing them out.*

- *Remember that frozen fruit will retain more moisture, so if you are using frozen fruit you will need to modify the recipe by halving the vinegar measurement.*

- *If you don't have a stick blender, you could press the sauce through a sieve to get a smooth texture, or blitz it in a food processor.*

- *Some dishwashers now have a sterilising option.*

- *There are a lot of hazards when you're preserving — the sauce is boiling and the bottles are hot — so I bottle sauce at night when my daughters are in bed.*

- *Use a jug to pour the sauce into the funnel. You can hold the handle as you dip the jug down into the pot, and the spout makes it easy to feed the sauce into the funnel.*

- *If you find you have one bottle that hasn't sealed, place it in the fridge and make it the first bottle you use.*

- *If you have more than one bottle that hasn't sealed, boil the mixture up again and repeat the sterilising process. Use a different lid as it may be damaged (especially if you are reusing bottles that you have collected).*

Spicy Apricot Sauce

3 kg (6 lb 12 oz) apricots

1 kg (2 lb 4 oz) onions

1.5 kg (3 lb 5 oz) sugar

1.5 litres (52 fl oz) vinegar

6 teaspoons salt

1 teaspoon ground cloves

1 tablespoon cayenne pepper

1 tablespoon ground ginger

My late mother-in-law would declare summer and early autumn 'squirelling' time — a time of year when you behave like a wee squirrel, frantically bottling and hoarding for the year ahead. We are lucky to have two beautiful apricot trees here on the station that are both always laden with fruit. There is an abundance to turn into sauce and preserves, and still plenty to give away.

This sauce is great to place in the picnic bag to serve with a slice of pie or use as an alternative to tomato sauce for sausages. I also enjoy using it in a leftover chicken sandwich.

Slice the apricots in half and remove the stones. Roughly chop the onions.

Combine all of the ingredients together in a large pot or jam pan and softly boil for an hour until the fruit is soft. Your house will smell amazing by this stage. Use a stick blender to make a smooth sauce.

Bottle the sauce while it is hot, using a funnel to pour it into hot, sterile bottles, and taking care not to burn yourself. Use a clean cloth to clean the rims before placing the lids on the bottles.

Leave the bottles to seal overnight. There is nothing more satisfying than hearing the lids go 'pop', signifying that they have sealed. Once the bottles have cooled and sealed, wash them in hot, soapy water to get rid of any sticky spots.

Tips and tricks

- During summer I freeze batches of fruit in 3 kg (6 lb 12 oz) bags, so that I can make sauce throughout the year.

- Freeze apricots in halves without the stones.

- Remember that frozen fruit will retain more moisture, so if you are using frozen fruit you will need to modify the recipe by halving the vinegar measurement.

- If you don't have a stick blender, you could press the sauce through a sieve to get a smooth texture, or blitz it in a food processor.

- Some dishwashers now have a sterilising option.

- There are a lot of hazards when you're preserving — the sauce is boiling and the bottles are hot — so I bottle sauce at night when my daughters are in bed.

- Use a jug to pour the sauce into the funnel. You can hold the handle as you dip the jug down into the pot, and the spout makes it easy to feed the sauce into the funnel.

- If you find you have one bottle that hasn't sealed, place it in the fridge and make it the first bottle you use.

- If you have more than one bottle that hasn't sealed, boil the mixture up again and repeat the sterilising process. Use a different lid as it may be damaged (especially if you are reusing bottles that you have collected).

Autumn

Getting everyone safely home

Two weeks before last year's autumn muster, on 25 March 2020, New Zealand went into a strict lockdown to navigate the Covid-19 pandemic. There was to be no movement between cities, towns and communities, and each home was to form a secure 'bubble'.

Farming, along with many other services that couldn't push pause, was deemed an essential service, and we had the task of creating an environment that was safe for our family, our staff and their families. The front gate was all but closed to traffic coming in, unless they were to transport or care for stock. Our staff's movements were restricted to avoid bursting the bubble.

We were incredibly lucky that over this time our local store provided a 'shop to door' service, which meant we could get groceries delivered without contact to our dwellings. Even though they sell food items, Warren and Dale wouldn't normally call themselves a grocery store, so they did a heroic job sourcing all sorts for our local farming and village families.

One Easter Bunny was very relieved when, after her online chocolate egg order was classed as an unnecessary item, Warren went out of his way to source

OPPOSITE: The golden road to the lakes.
ABOVE: Bill O'Donnell riding Canty with his pack team alongside.

chocolate eggs and bunnies so that our little people were not disappointed. Some of our bigger people were excited to find the Easter Bunny had visited the shepherds' quarters too.

The lockdown period presented another predicament: how was I going to shop for the autumn muster when I couldn't travel the hundred kilometres to the nearest supermarket in Oamaru? As well, I didn't want to risk exposing the station not least because we wouldn't be able to operate if anyone were to fall ill.

The shop for the muster consists of enough food for two weeks, for up to seven people. With a lockdown limit on grocery items (some people believed that the world would run short on toilet paper and paracetamol), I wouldn't be able to get more than two items at a time.

Luckily I had seen a local Facebook post about a bulk food service that would deliver to our gate. It wasn't an ideal everyday shopping service, because I try my best to avoid unnecessary packaging and prefer to fill up my baking jars and bins at a bulk food store in Oamaru called RealFood Pantry. But this service was a way around the item limits at the supermarket and could be delivered to the farm without bursting anyone's bubble.

Not only was sourcing food a problem, but sourcing staff was too. During the autumn muster we usually have several casual shepherds come from all over New Zealand to join the ranks. When the prime minister announced the impending lockdown, Hugh was quick to secure some casual staff who could arrive before the curfew. We were light on our usual numbers for the muster, but had enough to get the job done.

In total on farm we had thirteen people in four household bubbles who operated within the government guidelines — two metres' social distancing, no shared vehicles and strict hygiene.

Supplying smoko was a laborious task. I disinfected my kitchen surfaces each morning before I prepared any food. I wore gloves while cooking, and

OPPOSITE: A merino ewe among
the golden tussock.

each person received their smoko in separate paper bags that could be easily discarded. When smoko was dropped off or collected, it was handed over with gloved hands. It felt surreal to lose this human contact at a time that is usually quite social.

I lost count of how often I washed my hands or used hand sanitiser, and soon my hands became so raw that the skin would crack and bleed. When the country was in high demand for hand sanitiser, I was just trying to source a good hand moisturiser!

After two weeks of lockdown, and with no one showing any symptoms of the coronavirus, we were able to merge the bubbles and set out on the first week of the autumn muster. Although we were a little light-staffed, at least we were able to have everyone stay in the same hut, unlike a neighbouring property who had to divide their staff into different huts at quite some distance apart, with some musterers even sleeping on the porch to keep socially distanced. I pity the man who drew that short straw, as it's not uncommon to see snow on the ground at that altitude during this time of year.

TRADITIONALLY THE AUTUMN MUSTER is a much anticipated time of year when we gather up the flocks from the higher summer country and bring them home for the cooler months. We muster using horseback, foot and helicopter to cover the varying high country ground. Each of the seven or eight musterers relishes in the solitude and ceremony that is the autumn muster. Ours is divided into two weeks to cater for the different flocks: the Aviemore flock is about 10,000 sheep and takes five days to muster; the Otematata flock is nearer 15,000 sheep and takes six days.

The first year that I shopped for the autumn muster after Mandy's death, I remember the looks I got in the supermarket. I had parked up one trolley and had started on my second when I began to get funny little comments and looks. I sometimes wonder if the gap between rural and urban people has become so wide that people forget how rural communities live beyond town limits and can't visit the supermarket every other day, or perhaps it's not well known that the role of station cook even exists.

I have a muster grocery list saved on my computer that, as the years progress, I refer to and amend. After Joe and I married, I had been involved in a few musters as the packer, so in that first year I already had an understanding of what food was needed when camping out, and of course had some ideas of my own to add.

This year the stores, which can be prepared in advance, consisted of multiple cans of baked beans and spaghetti, three trays of eggs, fourteen loaves of bread, eight blocks of chocolate, ten kilograms of potatoes, and several kilograms each of carrots, onions, kumara, cabbage, apples and oranges — just to name a few of the bigger items.

Alongside the stores I also cooked and packed the following over the course of the two musters: curried sausages consisting of two kilograms of sausages, spaghetti bolognese consisting of two kilograms of mince, two roast beefs, two corned beefs, one corned venison, two fruit cakes, two batches of muesli bars, one large slice of rocky road, two double batches of chocolate-chip cookies, two double batches of chewy Anzac biscuits and two date loaves. Needless to say I need a break from my kitchen once everyone leaves.

At this time of year I also like to refresh the huts' first aid kits and make sure the cupboards are well stocked with candles, matches, rubbish bags and cleaning cloths for hunters who use the huts during the remainder of the year (and who now have no excuse but to leave the hut tidy). The station has many musterers' huts that over the years have been used in one way or another. Now of course we have the helicopter to help muster certain parts of the farm, and so stay-outs in those areas are no longer common. The two huts we still use on the autumn muster are called Glenbouie Hut (on the Otematata blocks) and Top Chimney Gully Hut (on the Aviemore blocks).

The first year I cooked on the muster, I remember one young shepherd nicknamed Beetle came in from a day mustering in the drizzle with chafing so bad his inner thighs were raw from wearing new Canterbury shorts that were stiff and unwashed. We searched the hut for anything that could make his next day bearable and found a tin of Rawleigh's — a liniment designed in the 1880s by William Thomas Rawleigh, a farm boy from Wisconsin, who wanted to make farmers' lives easier by bringing 'a little bit of civilisation' to people in remote areas. True to its design, the ointment did make Beetle's life easier, except for the fact that it was the menthol type of Rawleigh's, and so a sting was endured before relief. I now make sure that there is a tub of Vaseline or Rawleigh's in each first aid kit in every hut for any chafing misfortunes.

THE PACKER IS ESSENTIALLY the cook. The term comes from the days before trucks and farm vehicles were used on the muster, when the packer would be responsible for packing and securing supplies to the team of pack horses. At Otematata the horses, affectionately known as Prince, Wattie and Dobbin, would go ahead of the musterers and set up camp at each hut. By the time the musterers arrived, the hut would be warm and a hot meal ready to be served. Hugh remembers as a young shepherd that the first meal would often be saveloys and mashed potatoes.

The stores are now organised and packed by me. I bake and cook in advance, and the food is driven out with the team in the Land Cruiser along with the dog-tucker (sheep killed for dog consumption) and the chaff for the horses. *All* essential workers are well taken care of.

It is important to feed the dogs and horses just as well as the actual musterers. The days are long and physically demanding, and a good feed of carbohydrates, protein and nutrients refuels everybody for hard work the next day.

OPPOSITE: (Top left) The packer's utensils.
(Top right) My last entry in the logbook at Top Chimney Gully Hut.
(Below) Top Chimney Gully Hut nestled among the hills and briar.

To make things easier for the packer at the hut, I also prepare the first meal of the muster in advance. It often consists of beef (a step up from saveloys), and only needs to be heated up on the gas and served alongside some mashed potatoes. One reason I do this is because the old coal ranges in each hut require a good clean before you can get any real heat from them, and once they're going it takes even longer to get them up to temperature. Those ranges require a lot of love, care and attention throughout the day to keep them at temperature. If there is no breeze then you may as well admit defeat, because they need airflow to draw the flames.

Another reason I serve beef on the first night is because the rest of the week's diet mainly consists of mutton in some shape or form. That said, nobody complains — in fact my father-in-law quite enjoys this time of year when he can have mutton for tea each night of the muster.

WE FOUND OURSELVES a family of six over lockdown, when Mai (English) and Ruby (German) were stranded at the station leading up to the lockdown curfew. They were working on farm as part of a HelpX homestay experience and had little option of elsewhere to go. We were happy to offer them a safe haven, and they were happy to keep working as normal while the world was in such turmoil. Ruby, who became more homesick and worried for her family as the weeks went on, eventually got a repatriation flight home to Germany, but we kept Mai in our company well into lockdown level two. With our usual packer Tony unable to join us for the muster due to lockdown, Mai stepped up and became the packer for this year's Aviemore muster. It would have been quite unfair to send her out to Top Chimney Gully Hut with no experience or knowledge about cooking on a coal range, so we added a little Weber barbecue onto the packer's truck for her use. Each afternoon she would pop a roast mutton on a low setting and place the hood down to slow-roast the meat. When cooked she would rest it in the coal range to keep it hot, but she didn't have to worry about watching the range's temperature all day long. The little barbecue didn't take up much room on the packer's truck, and I can see it now being a regular fixture on the muster.

My years on the muster

The year after Joe and I married, and the year of Beetle's unfortunate chafing, my friend Jane Egden and I became the packers for the 2014 Aviemore muster. Mandy had packed the stores that year, and we embarked on our adventure determined to be the best cooks there had ever been in Top Chimney Gully Hut. I admit to being the world's worst gravy-maker, and Jane wasn't much better, but where we failed in gravy-making we excelled in pre-dinner snacks and pudding.

Prior to the muster that year there had been quite a lot of rain, which saw the Otematata River swell and take out the track to Top Chimney Gully Hut. Instead of following the winding track along the river from Forks Hut up Chimney Creek towards Top Chimney — a trip that usually would take 30 minutes — we had to take the high road over the Aviemore/Forks farm track and drop down to the hut, which took an hour. Time was not normally of consequence, except this year the wife of one of our casual musterers was due to give birth. Armed with a satellite phone in his saddlebag, Rob was prepared for a quick exit. On day two of the muster Rob arrived back at the hut with word that Sarah had gone into labour. Rob drove Jane and I out of the valley at a speed that only a soon-to-be dad would travel at, towards the river where we would leave him to walk up the washed-out track and pick up a truck we had parked there earlier in the week. Cellphone reception is sporadic that far out, and different spots pick up different networks. So it wasn't until the next afternoon that we received news that Henry Robert Waldie was born safe and well on 24 March, and Rob had made it in time.

Musterers are creatures of habit, and I remember that year how, while they didn't mind what was served for dinner, they were very particular about their breakfast. A banquet of mutton chops, sausages, bacon, eggs and baked beans was cooked up, devoured and washed up all before the men rode out each morning at six.

Lunch is the responsibility of the musterer. A range of baking, cold meats, fruit and bread is placed out for them to pack their own lunches. I am still amazed at how little they seem to eat and drink while covering such large distances each day. The distance varies for each musterer on their different beat, and is also determined by where the sheep are hiding, but on average a musterer covers ten kilometres per day over undulating terrain between 500 and 1500 metres above sea level. Quite often musterers return with their lunches intact, because if the sheep are moving that day then the musterers are too.

A few years ago we had an American girl randomly get in touch and ask Hugh for some New Zealand high country experience. She had been born and bred on a large cattle ranch in Wyoming and was in the country on her OE. Ali has since become a very good friend of ours after calling Otematata and the surrounding area home for over a year. Ali shared my concern for how little some of the older musterers fuelled their bodies while completing such an arduous task, something we felt had become a bad habit. If there was no time to stop and pour a cuppa from the flask, then that suggested they weren't stopping for a drink at all.

Ali formed many close friendships with those who worked with her, while sitting on rocks waiting for mobs to join up or the fog to clear. Discussing anything from world politics to different farming practices, she tried her best to educate the old fellas on identifying dehydration. But like they say, you can't teach old dogs new tricks. I can only hope that her advice fell on younger ears too. And whoever you ask, the answer to hydration at the end of the day is unanimous: beer.

Each morning on that muster with Jane, we would accompany some of the musterers in the truck to the furthest point of that day's beat with the

OPPOSITE: Breakfast is served
before the morning muster.

purpose of returning the truck to the hut, while the others left on horseback. A beat is the name given to the section of farm that is mustered that day. The musterers walk or ride one of the many station horses from one end to the other, sending their dogs out searching and collecting small mobs of sheep as they go. The horses are used regularly to muster, and are fit to handle the terrain. The musterers quite often have their own saddles that are well seasoned and comfortable, with saddlebags attached packed full of provisions — from lunch to wet-weather gear.

As one mob descends from the back of the property, they meet other mobs as the musterers come together. Merinos are creatures of habit and their whereabouts are quite predictable, so each year returning musterers have their own beats that they enjoy to work, as they know where the mobs will be hiding.

That was my first time venturing out to the boundary of the farm, and I loved sharing the experience with a good friend. When we weren't preparing meals, we were exploring, drinking plenty of tea, doing crosswords and having a good gossip.

Being able to complete an autumn muster on Otematata Station is on many young shepherds' to-do lists, and after being out there in the extensive high country I understand why. There is a sense of calm, and the fast pace of normal life seems irrelevant. For the shepherds, there aren't many who have walked those beats, and so those who do share a common bond.

Jane had to leave on the second-to-last day of the muster, and although she had grown up in a rural area near Temuka, the terrain on Aviemore was daunting for her to drive and made worse by the regular track being flooded out. Not far above Top Chimney Gully Hut was a closed gate on a steep incline which would test anyone's hill-start skills. But what amused me about Jane's departure was her mental and physical preparation for descending one of the valleys. On one particularly steep descent, she got out and walked it

OPPOSITE: (Top) The station horses at dawn.
(Below) Snow-capped hills above the Otematata River.

several times, summoning the strength to drive down. What made me laugh was that she was mentally preparing herself for a descent that wasn't part of the track, and had barely noticed a tight corner which followed. It wasn't until the final time she walked the track that she saw it — what I now fondly call 'Jane's corner'. She tentatively drove on. We had new perspective on Jane's heightened anxiety when, not long after, she found out she was expecting her first child.

THE NEXT AUTUMN MUSTER I was pregnant myself. Thirty weeks to be exact, and I remember Mandy's apprehension about me heading out to cook on my own, especially since there was no cellphone reception. I was determined to complete one last muster, as with a family on the way I wasn't sure I would ever get the opportunity again.

It was a fun week, with an author and photographer joining the team for the duration of the muster while working on a book called *Merino Country*. In total there were eight men and myself to feed on just two small gas hobs and a temperamental coal range.

As much as I had admitted defeat by bringing along packet gravy, most nights I was able to create a menu of roast mutton and veges served with either sautéed cabbage or cauliflower cheese, followed by pudding. It was quite the feast, especially on the night that I accidentally cooked enough rice pudding to feed twenty musterers. I'm not one to use measuring cups, and I often use my eye to measure ingredients. On the last evening, when I opened the packet of rice and poured it into my boiling milk, I wasn't expecting the packet to split and for the entire contents to be emptied into the camping pot. Determined not to waste the pudding, I simply added more milk and cooked up the largest rice pudding that Top Chimney Gully Hut had ever seen. More dogs than men enjoyed that course, and I'm not sure I've cooked rice pudding since.

The extra men working on the book also meant the sleeping quarters were full. I didn't mind, as I chose to sleep on the couch in the kitchen. Being in my last trimester of pregnancy I needed to pee a lot, and I didn't want to wake anyone up in the early hours as I padded my way outside in the frost to the long-drop — I left that to the team of snorers.

In the entrance to the sleeping quarters there is an old copper boiler used to heat water pumped up from the river. A 1930s petrol pump draws the water for both the tank outside the kitchen and the copper. One of the jobs of the packer is to light the fire under the copper and heat the water for the bath. So while the men were out mustering for the day I would sneak in a little bath before topping the copper back up with a few buckets from the creek, ready for the men to have a wash when they arrived back at the hut that evening. I never lingered in the bath for too long because I couldn't be sure when the first musterer would return, and since I was impersonating a beached whale at this stage, I wasn't sure how fast I could jump out of the bath if the hut door flew open. Six weeks later, and a month early, I gave birth to our first daughter, Flora — who was blissfully unaware that her granny had been right.

The Hughes 300

While I was working those musters as packer, Joe was 30,000 feet overhead flying his way to Queenstown in A320s for Jetstar. Today his involvement is also in the air, flying the helicopter. The Hughes 300 is a vital part of our autumn muster, as it cuts the time from a month to two weeks. The helicopter became a permanent station fixture in 1984 when Hugh had the idea of combining two of his loves — farming and flying — into one.

I first flew in the Hughes 300 not long after Joe and I met. I was just about to head overseas to work as a nanny in Italy, but that's not to say Joe didn't pull out all the stops to make sure I couldn't forget him. About a fortnight after we met, I was spending my birthday with a friend in St Bathans at Lauder Station. There wasn't great mobile coverage at the old homestead, and Robbie noticed that my phone had several missed calls. I stepped outside to find

some reception. It was Joe, wanting to know if there was an airstrip nearby he could land on. Robbie suggested the strip behind the Vulcan Hotel, and not long after I found myself sitting beside Joe in a powder blue and yellow Cessna 185 (an old Mount Cook Airline plane).

Joe's Scottish roots are strong, and he wouldn't normally be found spending money on frivolous things to impress a young lady. However, those same Scottish roots are what compelled him to take a detour from his trip to Dunedin Airport to pick up a young lass. After an airport sandwich and a day sitting in the sun while the plane was serviced, we were given the all clear to head home — but not in the Cessna. Instead, the Hughes 300 helicopter needed to be returned to the farm. It was a clever move from the young 23-year-old trying to woo the newly turned 27-year-old.

When it isn't being used to impress young women, the helicopter helps muster the steep hill faces. Merinos love to camp on the top of hills and venture downhill during the day. By sending the helicopter out early, well before the horses would reach those areas, Joe can search the steep face for stray sheep and muster them to the top of the hill where they will be gathered up with the main mob. Without the helicopter to muster this tough terrain, horses would be put through undue stress, more casual staff would be required to cover more ground, and longer days would be endured by all.

The helicopter has another integral part to play in the muster. If someone were to forget to pack the two trays of eggs for breakfasts, the helicopter can help redeem the cook's integrity by picking them up. Luckily for the cook her husband flies home most nights, so it's an easy fix.

The egg incident actually started a tradition in our family of an annual visit to the musterers' hut. On the second afternoon at Top Chimney Gully, Joe will fly in to make the following day's game-plan with Hugh. Together they see where the sheep are located for the next day's muster. This block is called 'Diggers' and covers steep faces that have been carved by the Otematata River

OPPOSITE: The Otematata River, winding
its way through the valley.

over thousands of years. Any sheep that have travelled as far as 700 metres down the steep terrain are encouraged upwards in the late afternoon.

Flying in the low autumnal light into Top Chimney Gully is intoxicating. I still get goosebumps each time, and feel a rush of pride to be associated with this remote part of New Zealand, which my husband's family has cared for and maintained for more than 130 years. How could I not get goosebumps, knowing that Joe and I are bringing up the sixth generation to continue a relationship with these mountains and rivers, their flora and fauna?

As we approach the hut it is already in the shade of the valley, having lost the sun behind the hill as a reminder that despite the clear skies we are now in autumn. The horses are rugged up in their paddock munching on well-earned chaff, and the musterers have begun to wind down for the day, feeding their dogs with beers in hand.

The girls are quick to explore the horse paddock, the kennels and the hut, and are even quicker to sit down with the team and devour the bags of chips that came out with the beers.

This year we flew into the hut on Anzac Day. I'd brought with me a wreath of rosemary for remembrance and some felt poppies the girls and I had made earlier in the day. I found myself thinking not only of those who had fallen in past wars, or those who might have served and then returned to the farm, but also more generally of the people who over the years have been a part of this incredible experience — an autumn muster at Otematata Station.

OPPOSITE: (Top left) A rosemary wreath hung on the hut door to commemorate Anzac Day. (Top right) Preparing for dinner at the hut. (Below) First on the boil is some water for brewing strong coffee and tea.
PAGES 174–175: Horses getting ready to ride out before dawn breaks at Top Chimney Gully Hut.

THIS IS THE LIST I work from for both the Otematata and Aviemore musters:

- piccalilli
- tomato relish
- gherkin relish
- mayonnaise
- tomato sauce
- Worcestershire sauce
- mustard
- 1 baking paper
- 1 lunch wrap
- 1 scrubbing brush
- 2 boxes of Steelo scourers
- sponge/scrubber
- aluminium trays
- rubbish bags
- chopping board
- tongs
- paper towels
- toilet paper
- 2 boxes of candles
- custard powder
- cornflour
- flour
- sugar
- 2 boxes of gravy sachets
- 1 bag of rice
- 1 salt grinder
- 1 pepper grinder
- 3 trays of eggs
- 14 loaves of white bread
- 6 bags of chips
- 8 blocks of chocolate
- 2 boxes of crackers
- 2 fancy cheeses
- 1 kg block of Edam
- 4 boxes of packet soup
- salami
- 2 roast beefs (cooked and chilled)
- 2 corned beefs (cooked and chilled)
- 2 corned venisons (cooked and chilled)
- bacon
- sausages
- mutton
- 4 cartons of beef stock (500 ml each)
- oil
- 6 cans of peaches
- 4 cans of tomatoes
- 10 cans of baked beans
- 10 cans of spaghetti
- 2 cans of beetroot
- potatoes
- cabbage
- cauliflowers
- carrots
- onions
- kumara
- apples
- oranges
- tea
- coffee
- Raro
- strawberry jam
- 12 baking items
- 2 first-night meals
- lightbulbs
- Panadol
- Savlon
- Vaseline

Cute Little Bread Rolls

350 ml (12 fl oz) warm water

4 teaspoons Surebake yeast

1 heaped tablespoon honey

600 g (1 lb 5 oz) high-grade flour

1 teaspoon salt

1 tablespoon oil

melted butter for brushing (optional)

I am no expert when it comes to making bread, or to working with yeast. I must admit to finding it quite daunting at first. But this recipe is exceptionally easy and the rolls come out fluffy and tasty.

I often use these in packed lunches, filling the rolls with cold meat, a dollop of Mary's Rich Red Plum Sauce (see page 142) and some homemade coleslaw.

Place the warm water, yeast and honey into your cake-mixer bowl. Mix with the spatula on a low speed until frothy.

Swap the spatula attachment for a dough hook. Add the flour, salt and oil and let the dough hook knead the dough for a good 10–15 minutes. I often set the alarm and go and do another task, checking every now and then to make sure the cake mixer doesn't walk off the bench.

Sprinkle the bench with flour and knead the dough into a ball. Place in an oiled bowl, cover and pop in a warm spot, and leave until the dough has doubled in size. This usually takes 45 minutes to 1 hour, but could be longer in cold weather — keep an eye on it and use your judgement. In my magic pot (see tips and tricks) it takes about 30 minutes.

Once doubled, punch down the dough, remove it from the bowl and form it into a snake. Cut the dough into 12 equal-sized balls. Gently knead, roll and shape each ball into a cute little bun.

Place the dough balls in a 3 x 4 arrangement in a roasting dish with sides, leaving a little space between each one. Leave to prove in a warm spot until doubled in size again, 35 minutes to 1 hour (or about 20 minutes sitting on top of a magic pot). Cover with a damp tea towel to avoid the dough drying out.

Preheat the oven to 200°C (400°F) fan-bake.

Once the dough balls have doubled in size, place in the oven and bake for 25–30 minutes until golden brown. Remove from the oven and brush with melted butter (this is optional, but oh so worth it) before allowing them to cool.

Tips and tricks

- *4 teaspoons of Surebake yeast is equivalent to 2 teaspoons of active yeast. If you are using active yeast you will need to allow time for the yeast to activate (about 15 minutes) before adding the rest of the ingredients.*
- *If your honey is creamed, heat it first so that it is soft and not firm.*
- *You could also make these by hand or on the dough setting of your bread-maker.*
- *I use the yoghurt setting on my magic pot (instant pot/ multicooker) to prove the dough. It really speeds up the process. Make sure to use a plate as a lid so that the dough doesn't rise through the valve on the pot lid.*
- *I use the yoghurt setting on my magic pot for the second rise as well, placing a narrow chopping board over the pot and the roasting dish on top of that.*
- *To keep filled rolls fresh in a packed lunch, pop a damp (not too wet) tea towel into a cake tin and place the filled rolls inside. Bring the corners of the tea towel together to cover the top before placing the lid on. They will stay fresh until lunchtime.*

Fruity Anzac Biscuits

Makes 20–24 biscuits

140 g (5 oz) butter

60 g (2¼ oz) golden syrup

80 g (2¾ oz) rolled oats

80 g (2¾ oz) sultanas

80 g (2¾ oz) finely chopped dried apricots

80 g (2¾ oz) desiccated coconut

80 g (2¾ oz) brown sugar

130 g (4¾ oz) plain flour

1 teaspoon baking soda

2 tablespoons boiling water

These are a chewy and fruity alternative to the traditional Anzac biscuit. Anzac biscuits originate from World War One, when the mothers and sweethearts of New Zealand soldiers would send them a batch of bikkies. The ingredients are said to not spoil, and so would last the journey by sea. In my kitchen these Fruity Anzac Biscuits have never lasted long enough to test that theory, but they make a nice twist on a classic.

Preheat the oven to 180°C (350°F) fan-bake. Line a baking tray with baking paper.

Place the butter and golden syrup in a pot over a low heat and melt together.

In a bowl, combine the rolled oats, sultanas, apricots, coconut, brown sugar and flour.

Dissolve the baking soda in the boiling water in a teacup.

Combine all of the ingredients and mix well. Use a pudding spoon to scoop the mixture up, and roll into balls. Place the balls on the prepared baking tray and use the back of a spoon to gently press each one down.

Bake for 12–15 minutes until golden. Store in an airtight container in a cool spot.

Tips and tricks

- *When I'm weighing the dry ingredients, I sit the bowl on the electronic scales and 'zero' them after each addition.*
- *If you don't have enough dried apricots, just double the sultanas.*
- *When I was testing the recipe, someone suggested that chocolate chips would make a great addition.*

Peppermint Slice

Makes 20 pieces

115 g (4 oz) butter

½ x 395 g (14 oz) can condensed milk

2 tablespoons cocoa

1 teaspoon vanilla essence

250 g (9 oz) packet wine biscuits

Peppermint Filling

2 cups icing sugar, sifted

2 tablespoons melted butter

2 teaspoons milk

2 teaspoons peppermint essence

Chocolate Icing

2 cups icing sugar, sifted

¼ cup soft butter

2 tablespoons cocoa

1 teaspoon vanilla essence

This is an all-time favourite of mine. A lot of peppermint slice recipes have solid chocolate toppings, which I don't like cutting into because I can never avoid cracking a few tops. With this recipe you don't have to worry about that, because it has a very delicious chocolate icing instead.

Line a 28 cm x 18 cm (11¼ in x 7 in) dish.

Place the butter, condensed milk, cocoa and vanilla in a pot over a low heat and melt together.

Blitz the wine biscuits in a food processor and place in a large bowl.

Pour the melted butter mixture over the biscuit crumbs and mix well. Tip into the lined dish and use a wet hand to press the base down to make an even surface. Place a piece of baking paper on top and use the back of a spoon to firmly smooth the surface. Pop in the fridge while you make the peppermint filling.

For the peppermint filling, mix all of the ingredients together in a clean bowl. Add boiling water, a little at a time, and use a knife to mix until you have a smooth paste. Spread over the base and place in the fridge while you make the icing.

For the chocolate icing, mix all of the ingredients together in a clean bowl. Add enough boiling water to make a smooth icing. Spread the icing over the slice and pop back in the fridge until set.

Once the slice is set, use a knife dunked in hot water to cut it into even pieces. Store in an airtight container in a cool spot.

Tips and tricks

- *This recipe is easily doubled (and who would complain).
  It's so tasty and no one likes a half can of condensed
  milk getting lost in the fridge.*

- *If you don't have wine biscuits, you can use any plain
  biscuit. I buy my biscuit crumbs from the bulk food
  store — that way I save on packaging and can get a
  large amount at once.*

- *To save time, you could melt the butter mixture in the
  microwave instead of in a pot on the stovetop.*

- *If you don't have a food processor to blitz the biscuits,
  place them inside a clean pillow case and smash with
  a wooden rolling pin. (I remember this being one of my
  favourite jobs as a kid.)*

- *If I have a biscuit-baking catastrophe, I will often blitz
  the biscuits and freeze the crumbs. They are perfect for
  reusing in a no-bake biscuit base recipe like this one.*

- *Sprinkle cocoa over the finished slice to make it look
  super-fancy for presenting to guests.*

Rocky Road Slice

Makes 25–30 pieces

230 g (8¼ oz) butter

395 g (14 oz) can condensed milk

¼ cup cocoa

2 teaspoons vanilla essence

500 g (1 lb 2 oz) wine biscuits

180–200 g (6¼–7 oz) raspberry jelly lollies, halved

1 cup raisins

180 g (6¼ oz) marshmallows, halved

handful nuts

500 g (1 lb 2 oz) chocolate, chopped

It has become a bit of a tradition to make this no-bake slice for the autumn muster. This year, the musterers did seem concerned that the supply was dwindling significantly each day while they were out working. Mai the cook mumbled something about large rodents, while looking quite flustered — and then later requested the recipe.

Line a large sponge roll tin, approximately 34 cm x 23 cm (13½ in x 9 in).

Place the butter, condensed milk, cocoa and vanilla in a pot over a low heat and melt together.

Blitz the wine biscuits in a food processor. Place in a large bowl with the lollies and raisins.

Pour the melted butter mixture over the biscuit mixture and mix well. Tip into the lined dish and use a wet hand to press the base down. Place in the fridge to set.

When the base is set, sprinkle over the marshmallows and nuts.

Melt the chocolate in a bowl set over a pot of boiling water, making sure not to let the bottom of the bowl touch the water. (Known as the double boiler method, this prevents the chocolate from burning.)

Pour the melted chocolate over the slice making sure to go back and forth across the entire slice. Use a spatula to evenly spread the chocolate without disrupting the marshmallows and nuts too much. Place in the fridge again to set.

Once the slice is set, use a knife dunked in hot water to cut it into even pieces. Store in an airtight container in a cool spot.

Tips and tricks

- *This recipe can easily be halved. Just don't forget about the half can of condensed milk in the back of the fridge.*
- *To save time, you could melt the wet ingredients in the microwave instead of in a pot on the stovetop.*
- *500 grams (1 lb 2 oz) is equivalent to two packets of wine biscuits. If you don't have wine biscuits, you can use any plain biscuit. I buy my biscuit crumbs from the bulk food store — that way I save on packaging and can get a large amount at once.*
- *If you don't have a food processor to blitz the biscuits, place them inside a clean pillow case and smash with a wooden rolling pin. (I remember this being one of my favourite jobs as a kid.)*
- *I like to use peanuts or cashews, but if you have plenty of walnuts at your place then they would work well too.*
- *If I have a biscuit-baking catastrophe, I will often blitz the biscuits and freeze the crumbs. They are perfect for reusing in a no-bake biscuit base recipe like this one.*
- *The slice is quite rich, so cut it into modest-sized pieces.*

Mary's Sultana Cake

Makes 1 cake (12–20 slices)

450 g (1 lb) sultanas

225 g (8 oz) butter, cut into chunks

3 eggs

350 g (12 oz) sugar

1 teaspoon almond essence (optional)

350 g (12 oz) plain flour

1 teaspoon baking powder

½ cup chocolate chips

½ cup chopped walnuts

Mary is Joe's grandmother, and this is her famous sultana cake. Whenever a tin of this is in the smoko bags, you'll be lucky to find any left at the end of the day, especially if Hugh, Gandy and Joe are involved. I've made this cake for every autumn muster I've cooked for, and it's always enjoyed by the old fellas, who I'm sure could survive on fruitcake and beer.

Mary's original recipe uses imperial measurements, which I reckon is part of its charm. I have added in the metric conversions in case you need them, but I recommend adjusting your scales to imperial if you can. It somehow tastes better that way.

Preheat the oven to 180°C (350°F) fan-bake. Line a 23 cm (9 in) square cake tin.

Place the sultanas in a pot. Add enough water to cover, then simmer for 15 minutes. Strain and return to the pot. Stir the butter through the hot sultanas and set aside.

Cream together the eggs, sugar and almond essence (if using) in a bowl, until pale in colour. Fold in the flour and baking powder, then fold through the sultana mixture.

Pour the batter into the prepared tin. Cover the top with chocolate chips and chopped walnuts.

Bake for 45 minutes.

Tips and tricks

- *The chocolate and walnuts are a must in my opinion, while the almond essence is optional.*
- *Use Sarah Paterson's tip for lining a square tin (see page 252).*

Apple Pie Filling

Makes 5 x 450 ml (16 fl oz) jars, or enough for 5 pies

8–10 large apples

juice of 1 lemon

1 cup water

1 thinly sliced lemon (skin on)

4 cups sugar

1 teaspoon ground nutmeg

2 tablespoons cornflour

2 tablespoons water

What's better than apple pie? Apple pie that takes hardly any time to prepare. This is such a tasty way to preserve apples — and the mixture smells incredible. Having some of this filling on hand makes hosting guests for dinner super-easy, as pudding is pretty much already made.

Wash, peel and slice the apples. Place in a large pot with the lemon juice and water, and bring to a rolling boil (one that when stirred can't be tamed). Reduce the heat and simmer for 10 minutes.

Add the lemon slices, sugar and nutmeg, and stir. Make a slurry with the cornflour and water, stir the slurry into the pot, and simmer for 1 more minute. Keep stirring until the mixture thickens.

Remove from the heat and transfer the mixture into hot, sterilised jars. Use a knife or an ice cream stick to stir the filling in each jar in a smooth circular motion to remove any air bubbles. Clean the rims with a clean cloth before placing on the lids and sealing.

Pop the jars in a water bath for 10 minutes to ensure the contents won't spoil on the shelf while waiting for you to enjoy them.

Tips and tricks

- *This recipe is easily doubled.*
- *To make the recipe gluten-free, use gluten-free cornflour or replace the cornflour with 6 tablespoons of pectin or 2 tablespoons of arrowroot.*
- *Use the method described on page 130 to sterilise your jars.*

Honey'd Pears

Makes about 6 x 950 ml (32 fl oz) jars

2 litres (70 fl oz) water

½ cup sugar

1 cup honey

6 'ish' star anise (I like 1 star in each jar)

juice of 1 lemon

5 kg (11 lb) of pears

We have two pear trees on the property. They're in the yard of an old house, so during the year they get no love or attention, and it's a bit hit and miss whether they bear fruit or not. But when they do, we are quick to get there before the possums scurry in.

Place the water, sugar, honey and star anise in a jam pan and bring to the boil.

While you wait for the syrup to boil, prepare a bowl of cold water with the juice of a lemon squeezed into it. Peel and quarter the pears, plunging them into the bowl of cold water as you go. This will prevent the pears from discolouring while you complete the rest of the batch.

Add the quartered pears to the syrup, and place a piece of baking paper over the top with a little hole cut in the middle for air. This will stop the pears from browning. Once the pears have reached a boil, turn off the element.

Pack the pears into hot, sterilised jars, seal and place in a water bath to process for 15 minutes.

Once the jars have cooled, remove the bands and check the seals. Wash them in hot, soapy water to get rid of any sticky spots.

Tips and tricks

- *I like to put a star anise in each jar to make them look pretty on the pantry shelf.*
- *Follow the instructions on pages 130–131 to sterilise your jars and to use a water bath.*
- *If you have jars that haven't sealed, either store them in the fridge for using up immediately, or reprocess them in a water bath.*

Winter

A new chapter

We often describe Otematata as a micro-climate. In the middle of winter when the valleys that surround us are engulfed in hoar frost, we will be standing on the plateau under blue skies, the sun warming the backs of the shepherds and my washing drying before the temperature drops off in the afternoon. Seeing the sun and basking in its warmth and light are vital when the winter days are short. We are so very lucky to live here.

After a cold frost, which can plummet to temperatures of minus four, or when the southerly whips through with a wind chill temperature as low as minus eight, the sun will pour into my kitchen window and stretch its fingers into the lounge. Our German short-haired pointer, Tulya, will compete with the girls for the sunny spots, where they'll curl up together with a book while I finish washing the breakfast and smoko dishes.

Last year all those lazy sun-snatching moments changed when Flora turned five on the third of June. Traditionally in New Zealand children begin school on their fifth birthday, although parents have until a child is six to enrol them in formal education.

Flora is a bright button and has always enjoyed learning. She is a sponge for

OPPOSITE: Evelyn sharing her smoko with Flora on the steps of the shearing quarters' kitchen.

all types of information and skills. Her memory never fails her, and she even remembers all sorts of things that Joe and I have long forgotten. But where she excels in her thirst for knowledge, she lacks confidence, so we decided to start her six weeks after her birthday at the beginning of a new term.

Sending your children off to school is a very emotional time. When you have your first child and people tell you to 'enjoy all the little moments because they grow so fast', you don't take in the entirety of what they mean until of course it happens. In the middle of the night when you are feeding a hungry baby, or you are consoling a toddler's tantrum, you never say, 'Wow these days are flying by.' But then it happens: your child turns five. You stop worrying about naps and new foods, and you're bribing them to wear a 'too blue' school uniform by adding pink hair clips.

I've recently been in contact with a dear lady who grew up here on Otematata Station. She was the cook's daughter and grew up here with her brother in the fifties, all through schooling and until she married. She is my go-to when I need to clarify any information about the station, and is the source of many a good story. We are very lucky to have Deirdre in our lives. In a weird twist of fate, we ended up in Timaru hospital together in 2020. I had damaged my knee while out running, and Deirdre was there baffling doctors on a third attempt to repair her gallbladder. When Flora started school, Deirdre sent me a poem that touched my heart. It's been floating around a while and I haven't been able to find the origin, but it summed up what everyone had been telling me:

Hold her a little longer
Rock her a little more
Read her another story
You've only read her four
Let her sleep on your shoulder
Rejoice in her happy smile
She is only a little girl for such a little while.

Now the sun-soaked mornings are a distant memory as we rush out the door to school. Despite a school bus being available, we decided to drive the 32-kilometre journey to school down past the picturesque lakes of Waitaki Valley, for the simple reason that safety is not a priority on school buses in New Zealand. If Flora were to ride the bus to school, I would be required by law to drive her to the bus stop in her five-point harness car seat, only to pop her onto the bus with no legally required safety restraint on an open-road stretch of state highway. Even though I am now winding an extra 640 kilometres onto the odometer each week and have effectively lost two hours from the day to driving, I just wouldn't forgive myself if something were to happen on that stretch of road with increased traffic from tourism and farming contractors.

There are some positives to this arrangement though. The little girl who is still anxious about school now has time to chat away any worries on the way there and back. Or we listen to audiobooks and podcasts, which is fantastic for the girls' oral language and literacy. To save Evelyn spending so much time in the car with me, she might instead spend time with Joe on the farm, and is becoming an expert on the winter feeding-out regime. At least one positive, I tell Joe in jest, is that I'm near the farm supply store two times a day for anything that needs picking up.

Throughout this new chapter of our lives, Evelyn has begun to shine. It is hard for a three-year-old to understand that pyjama mornings in the sun are now for weekends only, but she has acclimatised to our new routine relatively well. Her days are spent anticipating when Flora will arrive home, then not understanding why she hasn't been missed, what with Flora's classroom of friends. Without her big sister doing all the talking, I've seen Evie's personality develop into a real wee character, just as bright and fearless.

Driving long distances is something that those of us who live rurally are accustomed to. While Joe was away in England training to fly A320s, I taught in Papakaio near Oamaru and would travel a return trip of 180 kilometres each day from Otematata. In the mornings I would meet up with two girls,

Kylie and Genna, whose own boyfriends had brought them to the area, and we would carpool together down the valley to our respective jobs. Company made the daily trip more enjoyable, and I cherish the friendships that came from those kilometres.

On Mondays I would travel on my own to work, as I had hockey practice in Oamaru in the evening. On one particular Monday, the morning after Kylie's birthday, I was driving through Kurow when I saw her pull out behind me. She was flashing her lights and waving. I gave her a big friendly wave in return, and it wasn't until we were several kilometres down the road that I realised her over-zealous greeting was her telling me to pull over. As soon as I did, she was out of her car showing me her beautiful new engagement ring. Paddy had proposed on her birthday. Little did we know then that several years later we'd both be living in the Waitaki Valley with our eldest children starting school the same year, and our second children to follow in a few years' time.

NO FARMER WISHES FOR snow to settle too low on the hills, but we do cross our fingers and toes for a good base at our local ski field, Ōhau, only an hour from our front gate. We make sure to get as many days as we can up the mountain with Flora and Evelyn before shearing begins in late August. The girls have been learning to ski the past three years, and this year Flora finally found her feet. Evelyn is quite happy to try a few times on the learners' slope before being dragged around on the toboggan.

We usually leave home after Joe has finished feeding out the stock their winter balage. This is a crop of green grass harvested in the spring and baled into wrap, where it ferments and makes a sweet winter food source high in carbohydrates, which is great for the animals using extra energy to stay warm

OPPOSITE: Flora nibbling on some brassicas that have been grown
for the cows, while Evelyn observes from high on my shoulders.

or grow lambs and calves. Once we get our passes for the learners' slope, we usually ski for an hour before little bellies get rumbly and we stop for lunch.

I can't remember the last time Joe and I had a good day on the mountain ourselves or when we last left the learners' slope, but it's more about time together as a family. It won't be long before the girls will surpass us both in fitness and ability, and it'll be them wanting longer days on the mountain with their friends. By then I will be quite happy skiing a half-day and reading a book in the café.

From the carpark is the most spectacular view of the dark turquoise waters of Lake Ōhau and the open valley below. Pointing out of the water and breaking the skyline is Ben Ohau Peak — most recognisable from the Grahame Sydney painting.

Lunch is usually served from a heavy-duty canvas Susie bag on the tailgate of the truck. Joe and I like cold bacon and egg pie while the girls have noodles from their flasks. I also throw in a thermos of Milo, with marshmallows to plonk on top for extra energy. Throughout the carpark this scene is repeated, with some people even having little barbecues.

After lunch the girls will last another few hours before they are well and truly tired, and we head home. On the way down the mountain you can see all the way up Dobson Valley, a view that never ceases to amaze me. We promise the girls that if they make it down the mountain without falling asleep, there's an ice cream waiting at the Wrinkly Rams café in Omarama.

Scanning for bubbles

Just as winter settles in and the frosts become more frequent, we begin to think about the spring. Joe is heavily involved in pasture management on the property, and needs to ensure there will be enough feed grown to sustain our large breeding flock of merinos, the cattle and then the predicted number of lambs heading into the summer months.

We will have scanned the cattle for positive pregnancies back in autumn, around April. There are on average 350 cows to scan and it only takes one day in the yards at each property. A vet is employed, as the process involves a probe that is inserted internally to check for a healthy foetus. Any cattle that are dry are drafted off from the rest of the herd, and the pregnant cattle are given priority on which pastures they will graze. We want our animals to have the best available feed for growing healthy offspring. Another way we ensure a high rate of survival in the calves is to cross an Angus bull over our young Hereford cows. Angus and Hereford crosses are smaller to birth, and this will minimise stress on our first-time mothers.

The ewes are a larger operation, and this happens in winter. We have around 11,000 ewes to scan in just four short days. The reason for such a condensed timeline is that every other farmer also requires the same services. The scanner is one sought-after worker, and they have only a small window of opportunity to get around everybody's farms.

The four days of ewe scanning are long and usually quite cold. The yards in which the portable ultrasound machine is set up are relatively sheltered, but there's still frost underfoot. On these days I make sure there's a warm morning smoko and a large filling lunch so everyone stays well-fed. The food is picked up from my kitchen in the early morning by the young shepherds, and so I've had to get creative as to how to keep the smoko warm for a few hours before it is eaten.

There is, of course, the obvious choice of hot soup in the thermos. I like to send along a thick and hearty vegetable soup. I make it the night before in the magic pot, using dried red lentils and barley in the mixture to thicken it up. In the morning it is steaming hot, and I pour it into the thermoses as I prepare the smoko bags. I tried pumpkin soup last year, but got a bit of grief when it solidified in the thermoses and was hard to pour.

Another ingenious idea, for which I owe credit to Joe's cousin Erika, is to use a hot-water bottle. I place hot food like sausage rolls, bacon butties or little savouries in a metal cake tin, and then into an insulated bag with a filled hottie. This way the shepherds are able to enjoy a warm morning smoko while the frost still ices the ground.

One advantage of colder days is that I can make food without the normal worry of it spoiling, as a winter day in Otago is unlikely to get into double digits.

MOST OF THE SCANNING occurs at what we simply call our backyards, which hold so much character. The whole enclosure is made from stone and dates back to the 1860s. The yards themselves are made up of wooden-fenced areas that have been modified over the years for easy handling of the sheep. The scanner, Jeff, brings a little portable hut with him, and he sits inside the structure for the entirety of the day. His job is to scan each ewe and determine if she's carrying a lamb. Inside his little hut, Jeff has a monitor by which he can see the foetus, and a series of buttons to record the ewe's condition. This system is made incredibly easy with the introduction of EID ear tags. The electronic identification tags record each ewe that comes through the race. Jeff's equipment will note the number of lambs the ewe is carrying against her ear tag number, and this information is stored on a USB and later inputted into our farm management programme. The data is then used to determine where each mob will be placed, in regards to which feed will benefit it the most in the lead-up to lambing.

Ewes carrying twins are given preferential feed to nourish both the ewe and her lambs. The ewes carrying a single lamb are placed in a separate pasture. The ewes are later set stocked, which simply means that they are taken to their lambing paddocks in time for them to settle in before birthing.

If a ewe is scanned dry, she is drafted off and placed in a mob with others. The dries do get scanned again just to check there isn't a wee lamb hiding in the womb, and if they are carrying they get placed with their fellow mothers. Any ewes who aren't carrying will have a relatively easy spring and be mated

OPPOSITE: (Top left) Joe in his happy place.
(Top right) The girls love to go farming with Joe in the helicopter.
(Below) Rolling the chopper out of the hangar.

again next May. Any ewes who appear infertile after multiple years are either sent to our other property to be mated with a Suffolk sire (for meat production) or are culled. But this doesn't mean that they aren't useful to the farm: rather than providing us with replacement stock for our wool-growing flocks, or being mated with a more potent sire, they will still provide meat for the station, our staff and the working dogs.

When we use the Aviemore yards, which are not far from our house, I can pop by with the girls on the way home from school. From helping push the ewes up the race to the scanner's hut to peeking into the tent and watching the monitor, the girls are intrigued. Jeff, who was a new operator to the farm this year, not only thanked me every day for smoko and lunch (an instant favourite, in my books) but was incredibly patient with the girls. As each ewe approached the gate, he showed the girls what he was looking for in the ultrasound. He described each sac as a bubble, and helped them identify how many lambs a ewe was carrying. The girls would loudly announce how many lambs they could spot, and Jeff would press the corresponding number on his panel.

ON COLD, CLEAR DAYS the lakes look inviting with their glass-like surfaces, and if we haven't gone up the mountain then we try to take the boat out. We rug up like we would if we were going skiing, and pack a picnic. The lunch doesn't have to be flash, but what counts is getting off the farm for an afternoon. It is so important. It is too easy to continually see jobs that need doing and let the weight of the situation tire your shoulders. Each time we go out on Lake Benmore we like to explore somewhere new and go on small adventures. Flora and Evelyn always come home with little treasures bursting out of their pockets, their cheeks red and hair windswept.

One day this winter we boated all the way up the Haldon Arm to Black

OPPOSITE: (Top) My father-in-law, Hugh, with loyal dogs Midge, Doug and Roger. (Below) Waiting for the sun to lift and the frost to thaw.

Forest Station, where we holidayed one Christmas when I was heavily pregnant with Evelyn. Black Forest is extremely remote, and is accessed either by crossing where the Tekapo and Pukaki rivers meet when they are running low, or by driving in from Dog Kennel Corner near Tekapo. They have a range of comfortable and luxurious houses dotted along the shores of Lake Benmore, and one of our favourite summer holidays was when we rented a little cottage there. On visiting this winter, we pulled the boat into shore and toasted marshmallows on a camp stove (the Kiwi way around a fire ban) before racing home as it got dark.

Those trips to the lake are essential not just for Joe but for me too. Some days I feel I am always in the kitchen making food or scrambling into the truck to go somewhere. I get mum-guilt all the time when I ask the girls to wait while I finish a task. As much as the girls are wonderful at entertaining themselves, I want to show them that I can relax and have fun too. The look on Joe's face when we drive out the gate is often mirrored on mine. Every now and then, work on the farm can wait.

THE KITCHEN IS THE heart and centre of any home because of the warmth it offers guests. It's a place to welcome family and friends, to debrief, to laugh, to hang your children's art and give support. It's where the girls find me first thing most mornings for a snuggle and it's where we share our meals.

I have a good friend named Neil (aka Nelly), who I met while cooking in Western Australia. Nelly was one of ten men I cooked for while they seeded wheat one season. While travelling around the United Kingdom I ended up in his village of Harelaw, Scotland, and was instantly made to feel at home by his ma, Jennifer.

There was something special about Jennifer's kitchen. It was always warm from the Aga, and there was always a pot of tea brewing on the hot-plate. Throughout the day people would call in and the pot was topped up with fresh water or fresh tea bags. Nelly's family farm is an estate in the Scottish Borders where they milk 150 cows. The people who called in each day weren't ever expected, and could've been the neighbour, a worker or even the mailman. Actually, when Joe and I returned for Nelly's wedding to his sweetheart Emma, we were having a cuppa when the postwoman walked in and said to me, 'Well, you're back.'

One morning all those years ago while having a cuppa and a Tunnock's teacake with Jennifer, I was introduced to Nelly's Aunty Linda. Over another cup of tea, Linda told me that her son lived in New Zealand and was a shearer in Pleasant Point. I asked who he worked for and her answer was Adrian Cox. I asked if she knew where her son was working, and she thought for a moment. 'Oh, it's one of those place names that sounds like it repeats itself,' she said. Knowing that Joe was busy shearing at home, I suggested it could have been Otematata. And would you believe — while I was sitting in Jennifer's kitchen in Harelaw, her nephew was standing on the shearing board at my boyfriend's farm in Otematata, New Zealand. I guess two degrees of separation can apply outside of New Zealand too.

Jennifer's kitchen is still warm in my heart all these years later. Sadly she passed in 2018, and I often think about her when icing the girls' birthday cakes. Jennifer was frequently asked to ice many local wedding and birthday cakes, and I'd sit in awe as I watched her nimble fingers create fondant roses and flowers from memory.

AS WINTER COMES TO a close I am conscious of the lawns beginning to green up and grow, and that the vegetable garden needs attention. I often will have used old bales of balage that are no longer good for stock consumption to weigh down the garden beds for the winter months. Joe drops them off with the forks on the tractor and I unroll them in thick layers, hoping to stop the weed growth for as long as I can. (Make sure to wear gloves and a mask when

working with rotten balage. It can stain your hands and is bad to inhale.) I am still learning so much about gardening and, as much as my mum likes to impart her wisdom, I find I enjoy a bit of trial and error. Mum is constantly concerned about the amount of couch (or twitch) in my vegetable garden, but I remind her that even though it looks unruly, the vegetables continue to grow. One day when the girls are older, at school and more independent, I'm sure I will prioritise the garden a little more. Until then, I am reminded of some wise words my good friend Jane Millton once shared with me. Her granny used to say that while children are small, *they* are the flowers in your garden that need tending to, so enjoy them, and when the time allows your actual garden will still be there. I have to remind myself of this often. There will come a time when I can spend hours in the garden creating the landscape I dream of, but until then Flora and Evelyn are the wee blooms that hold my attention.

OPPOSITE: (Top left) Pack horse mamma in action.
(Top right) It's not a Milo without marshmallows.
(Below) Evelyn rugged up for a trip to see the cows.

FOLLOWING: The girls keeping warm while out on the farm.

Quick Salmon Quiche

Makes 1 quiche (6–8 slices)

Short Pastry

2 cups plain flour

½ teaspoon salt

125 g (4½ oz) butter, cubed and at room temperature

cold water

Filling

6 eggs

½ cup cream

½ cup milk

210 g (7½ oz) can salmon, drained and fluffed up

1 teaspoon Dijon mustard

chopped fresh parsley

salt and pepper

I know this is a contentious issue in most New Zealand farming households: *apparently country men don't eat quiche.* However, I have found that if no one says the word 'quiche' then somehow the issue doesn't exist.

Preheat the oven to 200°C (400°F) fan-bake.

For the pastry, rub the flour, salt and butter together to make a light crumb. Add small amounts of cold water at a time until a ball forms.

Handling the pastry as little as possible, gently roll out the pastry on a floured bench. Using your rolling pin, carefully lift the pastry into a quiche dish, fitting it to the base and sides and trimming off any excess pastry. Cover the pastry with baking paper, pour in rice or baking weights, and blind-bake the pastry for 10 minutes while you prepare the filling.

For the filling, mix all of the ingredients together in a bowl.

Remove the pastry from the oven, pour the filling over into the pastry case, and bake for 15–20 minutes.

Allow to cool before cutting and serving. If you are going to use the quiche in a packed lunch, make sure to cool and refrigerate before placing slices in the lunch bags.

Additional filling ideas

Cheese, asparagus and/or fresh cherry tomatoes from the garden would make great additions.

Tips and tricks

- I use the whisk attachment on my cake mixer to rub the butter and flour into fine crumbs. I then slow the mixer down and slowly pour the cold water in until the dough forms. (It doesn't take long.)

- If you're short on time you could use a 400 g (14 oz) block of store-bought short pastry.

- When I blind-bake any pastry casing I use the same piece of baking paper and the same batch of rice each time. Once everything has cooled down, I pour the rice back into a jar with the paper folded in a square on top to be used again next time.

- I made the mistake of sending my ceramic quiche dish out on the hill mustering one day and it came back in two pieces. I now cook the quiche in a loose-based round tin, remove it from the tin when it has cooled, and place it in a baking tin to send out.

- Set aside any excess pastry that you have trimmed off. When you get a chance, form it into a ball (handling it as little as possible) and roll it out again. Cut the pastry into squares and place a little dollop of raspberry jam on each square. Fold the corners up and pinch closed. Bake until golden and the jam is bubbling. The kids love to have them for pudding with a little custard.

OPPOSITE: Making sure smoko doesn't get left behind.

Two-ingredient Pizza Dough

Makes 2 large pizzas

4 cups self-raising flour

375 ml (13 fl oz) can beer

We all have those moments when we look at the clock and swear quietly because smoko has to be made super-fast, or because friends called in and all of a sudden it's teatime and the kids need to be fed. At times like those when the cupboards are looking bare, this recipe will save the day!

Preheat the oven to 180°C (350°F) fan-bake. Line 2 oven trays with baking paper.

Combine the flour and beer in a bowl and use your hands to bring it together into a soft ball. Add more flour if needed — you don't want it to be sticky.

Turn the dough out onto a floured bench, divide into 2 pieces, and roll out to your desired shape. Mine are often ovals so they fit onto long oven trays.

Transfer the bases to the prepared trays, then prick each base in a few spots with a fork. Top with your choice of toppings.

Bake for 25 minutes.

Topping options that work well for smokos
- *Caramelised onion relish, salami/bacon, cheese*
- *Tomato relish, ham/bacon, cheese*
- *Canned spaghetti, onion rings, cheese*
- *Ham/bacon, tinned pineapple, cheese*

Tips and tricks
- *If you don't have self-raising flour, replace each cup with 1 cup of plain flour and 1½ teaspoons of baking powder.*
- *If you don't have canned beer, use a stubby and make up the 375 ml (13 fl oz) with water.*

Savoury Scrolls

2 cups self-raising flour

90 g (3¼ oz) butter, at room temperature

pinch of salt

¾ cup milk

¾ cup tomato relish (or relish of your choice)

1½ cups grated Tasty cheese

½ cup chopped bacon or ham

These scrolls are so versatile; you can be as inventive as you like with the ingredients. And if you forget to get bacon out of the freezer, like I often do, it doesn't matter because the filling is just as tasty without it. The baked scrolls can be eaten straight from the oven, or cold from the smoko bag.

Preheat the oven to 180°C (350°F) fan-bake. Choose a dish with sides — the one I use is approximately 32 cm x 25 cm (12¾ in x 10 in) — and line it with baking paper.

In a bowl, rub together the flour, butter and salt until the mixture resembles fine crumbs. Add the milk and mix gently with a knife. Turn out onto a floured surface, sprinkle some flour on top and gently form into a dough. Roll the dough out into a rectangle about 1 cm (½ in) thick.

Spread the relish evenly all over, leaving a bare edge of about 2 cm (¾ in) so that when you roll it up none of the filling squishes out. Sprinkle the cheese and bacon over the top.

With floured hands, and starting from the edge opposite the bare edge, roll the dough up tightly into a log (the relish will help it seal). Trim the ends off the log to make it look tidy.

Cut the log into 12 equal slices and pop them into the lined dish with a gap between each one. Don't make your gaps too big, because you don't want the scrolls to spread too far — you want them to touch when cooked.

Bake for about 20 minutes.

Tips and tricks

- If you don't have self-raising flour, replace each cup with 1 cup of plain flour and 1½ teaspoons of baking powder.
- If you are getting your butter straight from the fridge, grate it to bring it up to room temperature.
- If you despise rubbing butter, like I do, place the scroll ingredients in your cake mixer and use the whisk attachment to rub the butter into fine crumbs.
- Baking the scrolls in a dish with sides helps to avoid them spreading too far. You want them to touch when cooked, but not to be squished. You could also use a muffin pan, placing one scroll in each hole.
- Other ingredients that taste good include spring onion, sun-dried tomatoes, caramelised onions, spinach, pesto, chopped herbs or feta.

Soft Cinnamon Scrolls

120 g (4¼ oz) butter, softened

¼ cup brown sugar

2 teaspoons ground cinnamon

3½ cups self-raising flour

1 cup cream

1 cup soda water

½ cup caster sugar

White Icing (optional)

boiling water

1 cup icing sugar

If I can make a well-loved recipe in a handful of quick steps, then I know it will be a successful option for smoko. These super-soft and super-easy cinnamon scrolls are great for when you are time-poor, as you don't have to wait for the dough to prove. They are also delicious with or without the icing — you choose.

Preheat the oven to 200°C (400°F) fan-bake. Choose a dish with sides — the one I use is approximately 32 cm x 25 cm (12¾ in x 10 in) — and line it with baking paper.

Cream together the butter, brown sugar and cinnamon and set aside.

In a separate large bowl, place the flour, cream, soda water and caster sugar. Use a butter knife to gently mix everything together, forming a soft dough.

Tip the dough onto a well-floured surface, and sprinkle a little more flour on top. Roll the dough out into a rectangle about 1 cm (½ in) thick.

Spread the creamed butter mixture over the dough. Don't press down — it should spread like an icing.

With floured hands, roll the dough up tightly into a log. Trim the ends off the log to make it look tidy.

Cut the log into 12 equal slices and pop them into the lined dish with a gap between each one. Don't make your gaps too big, because you don't want the scrolls to spread too far — you want them to touch when cooked.

Bake for about 20 minutes.

For the icing (if using), mix 1 tablespoon of boiling water at a time into the icing sugar to make an icing with a smooth pouring consistency.

Allow the scrolls to cool a little before you ice them. Drizzle the icing over the dish of scrolls, using a sweeping motion as you move your hand back and forth across the dish.

Tips and tricks

- *If you don't have self-raising flour, replace each cup with 1 cup of plain flour and 1½ teaspoons of baking powder.*
- *Keep a stash of UHT cream in your pantry to use when you don't have any fresh cream.*
- *If you don't have a SodaStream, use store-bought soda water or lemonade — but consider purchasing cans that can be recycled easily, rather than plastic bottles.*
- *If you use lemonade, omit the sugar.*
- *Baking the scrolls in a dish with sides helps to avoid them spreading too far. You want them to touch when cooked, but not to be squished. You could also use a muffin pan, placing one scroll in each hole.*
- *For an alternative filling use raspberry jam and a sprinkling of chocolate chips.*

Forgotten Fruit Muffins

2 cups self-raising flour

½ cup sugar

1 egg

½ cup oil (mild flavour)

1 teaspoon vanilla essence

1 cup yoghurt

1 cup chopped washed fruit

Topping

1 tablespoon brown sugar

handful rolled oats

few chopped walnuts (optional)

I call these Forgotten Fruit Muffins because in Otematata Village, which is a popular holiday destination, people leave their cribs to head back to work just as the fruit is beginning to ripen. The fruit is often forgotten and left to drop. I have made friends with a few crib owners now who let me forage their trees for fruit. I often freeze it so I can make these muffins in winter to remind us of warmer months.

Preheat the oven to 180°C (350°F) fan-bake. Line a 12-hole muffin pan with paper cases.

Place the flour and sugar into a bowl.

In another bowl mix together the egg, oil, vanilla and yoghurt.

In a third bowl mix together the topping ingredients.

Combine the flour mixture, the egg mixture and the fruit, and very gently mix together. Spoon the batter into the paper cases. Sprinkle some of the topping on each muffin.

Bake for 25–30 minutes.

Tips and tricks

- *If you don't have self-raising flour, replace each cup with 1 cup of plain flour and 1½ teaspoons of baking powder.*
- *You can use any flavour of yoghurt. I like to use up the yoghurt in the bottom of the container that the kids won't eat because it's gone all gloopy.*
- *Any type of fruit works well. You could use apricots, nectarines, peaches, bananas, rhubarb, apples, pears, raspberries, black currants or feijoas.*

Station Brownie

Makes 20 pieces

125 g (4½ oz) butter

¾ cup brown sugar

¼ cup caster sugar

225 g (8 oz) dried fruit

150 g (5½ oz) self-raising flour

1 egg, lightly beaten

This brownie is chewy and sweet, with a hint of caramel. It will keep in an airtight container for up to 10 days — that's if it's not devoured straight away.

Preheat the oven to 190°C (375°F) fan-bake. Line a 28 cm x 18 cm (11¼ in x 7 in) brownie tin with baking paper.

Melt the butter in a pot. Add the brown sugar and caster sugar, and dissolve them into the butter.

Allow the mixture to cool, then add the dried fruit, flour and egg, and stir to combine. Pour the batter into the lined tin.

Bake for about 20 minutes until golden on top and firm to touch. You want the brownie crunchy on the outside and chewy on the inside.

Allow to cool before cutting into pieces.

Tips and tricks

- *This recipe is easily doubled.*
- *Use any dried fruit you like — a combination or just one kind. I often use raisins.*

Throughout
the seasons

On reflection

Sometimes when you look back on your journey, you realise you have become more than you expected. The journey I'd imagined for myself did not end — it just changed direction.

I married Joe on a bluebird day with clear skies and sweltering 35-degree heat. We were surrounded by all the people we knew and loved, whom we had shared so many adventures and memories with. Over the years, friendships and connections had defined my character and influenced my life. Our wedding was one bloody big party to celebrate!

However, that day showed us that life never goes to plan — you simply have to take what it gives you, surround yourself with people who make you happy and embrace the awkward bits, as it's those that make the best memories.

Mum had embroidered *18 January 2013* on the bottom of my dress in blue thread next to my late father's friendship ring, incorporating something new, blue and old. Our close friend Craig, who had first introduced me to Joe in the Kurow pub after a day at the races, flew us in his helicopter with the registration HEN, which held many memories for both our parents and

OPPOSITE: Totara Peak in early spring.

had connected us long before we met. We got to share the day with my sister Christy, who we lost eight months later to cancer, and Joe's mother, who we lost four years later.

We were married in St Thomas' Church in Omarama. Joe's father piped me down the aisle as I walked with Mum, arm in arm. The church has a glass ceiling above the altar, and before long the boys were feeling the heat. We were only partway into the ceremony when one of the groomsmen, Henry, fainted — twice.

The minister, who may have had a few tipples to calm his nerves before officiating his first wedding in nearly twenty years, called my mum 'Philippa', offended my soon-to-be mother-in-law, called Joe's sister Olivia 'Olive', and referred to Joe as 'Yoseph' throughout the ceremony (a nickname I now often call Joe). But once we'd adjusted to all the nerves and the heat, it was me who had people laughing. That morning while getting ready, I'd been wondering how I would respond to my vows. Would I say 'I do' or just simply say 'yes'? Instead, to a raucous response, I blurted out a 'Yes, please' — always one for my manners.

At that moment we could never have known what was in store for us — career changes, family losses, the heartache of not being able to start a family easily, the heartbeats of our newborns and eventually my becoming a high country cook. But year by year, as the seasons changed, what stayed constant throughout was the land that tied us all together.

It's land that has brought home five generations of family to fulfil their duty of care, to enrich the earth and continue to provide sustainable resources for the future. I want our girls to feel this connection. I want them to feel proud in their role as caretakers of the land and to protect the values they are raised with. Some would call it a simple life, but I disagree. It is a rich life.

OPPOSITE: (Top left) Flora sampling the broccoli.
(Top right) A race to feed the chickens some broccoli leaves.
(Below) The girls always take delight in feeding hungry lambs.

Essential items for your pantry and kitchen

A well-equipped kitchen is vital, especially if you live remotely. These are some of the items I find key for a filling smoko or lunch, even if the cupboards are beginning to look a little bare. With these staples below you will be able to make most of the recipes in this book, or a version of them.

My pantry staples

- butter
- cheese
- eggs
- New Zealand-grown standard flour
- baking powder
- UHT cream
- powdered milk
- tinned smoked salmon
- jam
- relish
- beer

My kitchen tools

- icing knife
- good paring knife
- good serrated knife
- great vegetable peeler
- set of accurate measuring cups
- set of accurate measuring spoons
- electric scales that use both metric and imperial settings
- old-school scales (which I use for preserving, as I often measure the fruit as I prepare it and the electric scales will time out)
- dough scraper (perfect for scraping dough off the bench)
- cast-iron fry pan
- cast-iron pot
- free-standing cake mixer
- SodaStream machine
- Nespresso or similar coffee-maker
- yoghurt-maker or the means of making your own yoghurt
- magic pot (what I call my multicooker or Instant Pot)
- Susie bags (a brand of canvas bags for packing up smokos and lunches)

What's up your sleeve?

When you live remotely for long enough, you begin to keep tricks up your sleeve to get you through any number of situations. Before inheriting the role of cook I had very little up my sleeve, but over the past few years each of the little tricks below has become standard household procedure. And I've come to find that if I don't have the answer, someone else will. Since starting my Instagram **@whats_for_smoko,** I have found a sense of community among other rural cooks and household executives, who are always willing to share their favourite tips. At the end of this list I've left a space for your own tricks, or for any you might pick up from friends and neighbours.

Butter paper

I go through a lot of butter, and as a result I have a lot of papers left over that I use to line my loaf tins. They should fit perfectly lengthways. You could butter the ends of the tin, but I find running a knife down the ends of the cooked loaf helps tip it out.

Chopping board above the chook bucket

This is one to put on your kitchen wishlist. Above my drawer for the food scraps and rubbish bin is a pull-out chopping board, something that was quite common in older style kitchens except that I have added a cut-out hole at the end above the food scrap bin. As I peel or chop off the ends of the vegetables, the waste goes down the hole into the bin.

Citrus peel

Chickens and pigs don't like to eat citrus peel, and you can't put them in worm farms either. I keep a jar of citrus peel in the freezer and, when it's full, I fill it with white vinegar and leave on the bench for a week. Strain the liquid and make up a kitchen spray using a 50:50 solution of the citrus vinegar and cooled boiled water. You can even blitz the discarded peels in a blender to use as a cleaning scrub.

Dish cloths

Disposable dish cloths are essentially plastic. You may be able to wash them, but each time you're introducing little bits of plastic into our water and waste systems. I prefer to use cotton dish cloths. You can buy really cute knitted and crocheted ones from small home businesses or, like my mum, cut up old towels. You can overlock the edges so they look tidy and don't fray.

If your dish cloths begin to smell after a normal wash, simply boil them in a pot with a tablespoon of washing powder or washing liquid and a good glug of white vinegar. You will be surprised at the colour of the water after half an hour. Line-dry to use the power of the sun to disinfect ('an hour in the sun and then it's done') or even hang in a frost (not many bugs live below zero degrees).

Dropping a pumpkin

Instead of cutting into a whole pumpkin and endangering my life, I simply hold it on its side above my head and drop it on concrete with a little force. It will break evenly in two every time and makes cutting slices easier.

Eggshell pieces in your baking

If you have a piece of eggshell break into your bowl while baking or cooking, use the bigger shell to scoop the broken piece out with ease. If you use your fingers, it often bounces all around the bowl.

Freezing cookie dough

Each time you bake biscuits (or cookies), double the batch and roll into balls as normal. Bake half the amount of dough and place the rest in the freezer on baking trays. Once frozen, free-flow in a bag (I use old bread bags) and save for a quick bake another day. Place on your baking tray to thaw before baking, and cook as normal, following your recipe. Alternatively you could bake one or two at a time to have with a cuppa when you deserve a wee treat.

Freezing eggs

If you have chickens and can't keep up with the daily eggs, freeze them for when the chooks go off the lay in the cooler months. Crack the eggs into silicone muffin trays and freeze. Once frozen, pop them out of the moulds and free-flow in a container before returning to the freezer for when you need them. Once thawed (the yolk can be quite jelly-like), they are fine to bake with or pop in a quiche. Alternatively you could whisk up the amount you use in your quiche recipe and freeze. Simply thaw and add the remaining ingredients for an easy lunch. I wouldn't suggest frozen eggs for poaching.

Frozen water pipes

For those of us in areas that freeze overnight, it's important to make sure your pipes are insulated for frosts. As well as lagging pipes, you can leave a tap dripping overnight in the coldest parts of the house, or alternatively pre-set your washing machine and dishwasher to come on at different times in the early hours. This way, water is flowing through the coolest hours of the night and early morning, and will keep the water from settling in the pipes long enough to freeze. Each winter Joe reminds me daily to make sure I detach the hoses from the outside taps after use, too. This will drain the hose and help with its longevity — a hose can split when water expands in a frost.

Grated eggs for sandwiches

Six hardboiled eggs make enough filling for a loaf of sandwich bread. This is an essential tip if you ever find yourself having to cater for team lunches. Save yourself a lot of time and trouble by grating the eggs before adding mayonnaise (or whatever you use to make up your egg mixture). It's much easier than mashing, and you won't get lumps of egg white.

Hard brown sugar

If you find your brown sugar going hard from being exposed to air, simply place a crust of bread in the container and it'll be soft again the next day.

Hay bale glasshouse

The winter prior to this I didn't have a glasshouse, and I was given this suggestion to lengthen the growing period for my vegetable garden. I found a large old window on the farm and made a surrounding wall of little hay bales to the exact measurements of the window frame. I then planted some late lettuces and brassicas, and placed the window frame on top. The plants were well insulated from the elements and we were still eating lettuce in June, which is unheard of for most Otago garden beds.

Hot water bottle

A hot water bottle can keep savouries warm until morning smoko. Place a hottie on the bottom of a thermal bag (like a supermarket cooler bag) and place the container with the savouries on top. It's quite nice to offer something warm on the hill after a big frost.

Instant pudding

I like to use vanilla instant pudding as the filling in my chocolate éclairs. I make up the packet using one cup of cream and one cup of milk. You can make it ahead of time and leave in the fridge until filling the casings.

Ironing tea towels

Now this may seem excessive, but hear me out. With emergency services a long way from home in rural areas, it's essential to have a good first aid kit on hand for any emergencies. I like to iron tea towels to place in the smoko room, and keep one at home, as a sanitised item to have on hand. If you need to stem any bloodflow, a tea towel can be found alongside the first aid kit in the smoko room and taken to the accident site. The ironed tea towel will minimise infection and the heavy-duty cotton will absorb the blood. They can also be used as a sling or to cleanly tie off splints.

Keeping sandwiches fresh

It's been quite some time since I have used clingfilm in the kitchen. If I've made sandwiches or filled rolls for packed lunches, I simply lay a damp tea towel on the bottom of a cake tin and pack the cut sandwiches tightly inside. I use the remainder of the tea towel to cover the sandwiches. They will stay fresh as long as the tea towel is damp.

Kitchen scullery

This is a dream scenario, but if I could design the ultimate kitchen scullery then this is what I would like. It would begin with a door facing my vegetable garden so that I could step inside with my picked produce. There would be a large concrete tub with a bendy hose for washing the produce, and a rack hanging over a third of the basin for the clean vegetables to drip-dry on.

There would be a walk-in chiller for storing meat, with a granite benchtop outside the door for preparing the meat. Above the benchtop would be a magnetic strip for hanging the knives.

In a different area would be my cake mixer on a benchtop just for baking. Below the bench there would be pull-out bins for bulk storage of flour and sugar. In this area I would also have a basin and dish-drawer for rinsing and washing any equipment as I baked.

There would be ample storage, and of course a door to close if visitors arrive and I need to hide the mess.

Leftover icing

If you find you have leftover icing, freeze it for another day. Once thawed, use a little boiling water to bring it back to the desired consistency.

Leftover mince

After we have had spaghetti bolognese or nachos, I keep the leftover cooked mince to use in scrolls. Roll out flaky puff pastry and spread the mince over it. Roll up and cook at 200°C (400°F) for 15 minutes for an easy hot smoko.

Leftover stews and casseroles

Any leftover stews and casseroles are kept to use in little pastry pies. I have a cheap pie-maker from Kmart that makes quick work of this. There is usually a large amount of gravy left over too, which I often freeze, and if Joe is home on his own he will thaw some for a quick tasty gravy to go with sausages.

Leftover wine

Leftover wine may not be a problem in your household, but perhaps you've had a party and have collected a few stray bottles. Pour the wine into containers and freeze for use in stews and gravy.

Lining baking tins

There are many ways to line a baking tin. These are the methods I use most often. I also make sure to reuse the baking paper as many times as I can before discarding.

- **Lining a square tin**: Sarah Paterson from Armidale in Maniototo taught me this method. Cut the exact length of baking paper and lay it across the length of your tin. Now cut the exact width of baking paper and lay the other way, making sure each time you have enough to cover the sides.

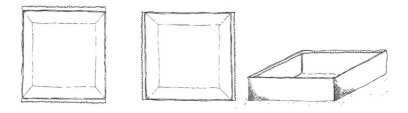

- **Lining a loaf tin**: Use a wrapper from a block of butter to lay across the length of your loaf tin.

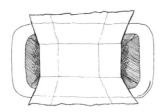

- **Lining a sponge roll or brownie tin**: Cut a piece of paper larger than your tin. Pinch the corners, fold down the wee triangle of paper and press down to make a box shape.

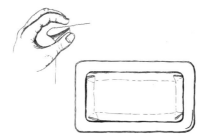

- **Lining a circle tin**: Fold a square of baking paper diagonally. Fold diagonally six more times. Next measure the distance from the middle of your tin to the outside (the radius) and cut with a pair of scissors. Unfold your circle and place at the bottom of your tin. You could grease the side of your tin with butter or line using strips of baking paper secured with a little butter, kitchen spray or coconut oil.

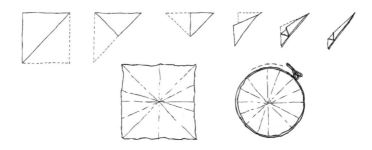

- **Lining a round spring tin:** With the round removed, place a square of baking paper over the bottom of the tin. Press the round down over the paper and wriggle until the bottom fits into the grooves of the spring tin. Close the spring function to get a tight seal and the bottom will be secure and lined. You could line the sides using the methods described in 'Lining a circle tin' above.

 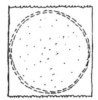

- **Jamie's scrunch technique:** Rip a piece of baking paper big enough to fit your tin and scrunch it up into a ball. Un-scrunch it and place it into your tin, pressing down into the corners. To get a better fit you could wet the paper first and then scrunch.

- **Flour technique:** To avoid baking paper altogether you can simply grease your tin using butter or coconut oil, making sure to cover the entire surface. Place a little flour in the tin and move it around to cover all of the greased area. Tip out any excess flour, and it will be ready to pour your batter into.

Milk powder

I keep powdered milk in the pantry for those baking emergencies when you run out of fresh milk. Four tablespoons of milk powder make up a cup of milk. This is also handy for when you are low on fresh milk and would rather keep it for drinking. Use powdered milk in your baking instead.

Old cake tins

I started using old cake tins in the smoko bags for several reasons. One was that Hugh ran over the smoko bags and crushed our plastic containers. Plastic often can't be recycled and is essentially waste when broken, whereas if the tins are squashed they can be shaped back or dropped at a scrap metal shop. I also find that whoever I'm feeding tends to unload the tinned smoko and lunch properly, because they can't see in and pick out their favourite slice from the top. I mostly find these old tins at secondhand stores.

Prepping mousetrap mixture

When you're making smoko and lunches that leave the kitchen at five-thirty in the morning, you learn to prepare as much as you can the night before. I find prepping the mousetrap mixture the night before and storing in the fridge can save a lot of time.

Preserving methods

When it comes to starting your preserving journey, buy or get out from the library the *Ball Complete Book of Home Preserving* and follow along to ensure good preserving and canning methods.

Ring tin replacement

If you don't have a ring tin for a specific recipe you can use a glass jar (greased with butter or coconut oil) and place it in the centre of a round tin.

Rising bread dough

I find it hard to rise bread consistently in the cooler months, so I place my dough in the magic pot (multicooker) on the yoghurt setting. The heat is low enough that it doesn't dry out or cook the mixture. Place a plate over the top instead of the lid, as you don't want bread to rise through the valve. I also prove my second rise on the magic pot too. I place a wooden board over the pot and on top place the dish the bread will be cooked in. Using the yoghurt setting again, I just drape a tea towel over the top and find it's doubled in no time.

Rubbing butter

I dislike rubbing butter for scones, pastry or crumble, so Joe's cousin Jess taught me to use the whisk attachment on my cake mixer. I simply chop the butter into small pieces and add to the mixer with the dry ingredients. Whisk until the consistency of fine breadcrumbs.

Scraping the bottom of the cake mixer bowl

If you find your cake mixer doesn't reach the bottom of the bowl while creaming butter and sugar or when mixing small amounts, lean on the top for a wee while to get the blade down a little further.

Shaping scrolls and pinwheels

If you find your scrolls and pinwheels tend to spread too far, you could use a lined sponge roll tin or your muffin tin. If cooked in a sponge roll tin you can serve them as a pull-apart, or alternatively place individual slices in your muffin tin for perfect round pinwheels.

Silicone liners

I use silicone mats to line my baking trays and lessen the amount of baking paper I use in the kitchen. I purchased the largest size I could get and found that, when I cut them to size, the leftover pieces were the perfect fit for my

brownie tins. When you are looking for silicone liners, make sure that they are a high food-grade product so you can use them safely for many years.

Square tin alternative

If you don't have a square tin for a specific recipe, you can place a loaf tin in the width of a large sponge roll tin to create a space like a smaller square. Line as you would a normal square tin.

Stainless-steel benchtop

When we moved to the farm, I was lucky enough to make some changes to the cottage kitchen and bathroom area. One of the first things we invested in was a stainless-steel benchtop (influenced by my friend Becs at Lauder Station). I can place any hot trays or dishes directly onto the benchtop without it marking. I make scones and shape bread on this surface, and then use a dough scraper to scrape off the pesky flour mixture. I can cut on it and, even though it marks, it adds to the character of the kitchen. The girls play with playdough and glue crafts on it, and it cleans up perfectly.

Sterilising jars and bottles

There are several methods for doing this, but I like to wash the jars and bottles in hot soapy water before placing them in a hot oven. You can now get dishwashers with a sterilising function, which might be worth looking into when you need an upgrade. If you're looking for alternative methods, the guidelines in the *Ball Complete Book of Home Preserving* are based on decades of preserving knowledge.

Sticky labels

If you use recycled bottles and jars for your preserves and you want to remove the labels first, you could try this method. Warm the bottles with tap water while you boil your kettle. (You don't want the bottles cold as this may cause them to crack.) Tip out the warm water and carefully pour the boiled water into the bottles. Leave for a few minutes to soften the glue on the label. Carefully pull off the label, starting in the corner. If the label doesn't come off cleanly, rub some lemon or eucalyptus oil onto the stubborn bits and scrub with a kitchen scrub. Give it one last scrub in hot, soapy water before sterilising for bottling. Alternatively you could use a lemon Steelo pad to get off any stubborn glue.

Sugar cubes

Instead of using loose sugar in a jar in the smoko bags, I use sugar cubes. They're handy for many reasons: no one can double-dip a wet spoon into the loose sugar, making the crystals stick; it's much easier to clean up if someone doesn't put the lid back on the jar properly; and the workers can slip one in their pockets as a treat for their horse.

Tea towel over the cake mixer

To stop dry ingredients poofing up and out of your cake mixer bowl when mixing, hold a clean tea towel over the top of the mixer and down the sides of the bowl. Hold tightly until the mixture has begun to combine.

Transporting iced cakes

It can be quite messy fitting a freshly iced cake into a cake tin, especially if you're keeping it whole. Place the cake onto the lid of the cake tin and place the tin itself on top. I often use a whiteboard marker to write 'This side up' so that no one makes the mistake of tipping it upside down.

Walking cake mixer

I have trouble with my cake mixer walking off the bench when it's kneading dough. You could pop a tea towel or anti-slip mat underneath, but it's more fun to put a can at the edge of the bench. If you hear the can hit the ground then you know that the cake mixer is close to going over too.

Your favourite tricks

Do one thing

Doing 'one thing' is the action of making changes in your home and on the farm just one thing at a time, working towards living more sustainably and minimising waste. They may seem like small actions, but it isn't long before they add up. You can feel proud not just because you have made the changes, but because your family and friends will begin to see and adopt them too.

The thought behind doing one thing is that some people find the complete ideology of living sustainability daunting. By changing and maintaining just one thing in your home to start, that decision can lead on to other 'one thing' actions. Before you know it, you are making conscious decisions on a regular basis. And by starting in the home, you will soon see opportunities to extend changes to the farm too.

These are just some of the things that I have begun to change in the home over the past couple of years, and some of the things Joe and I have begun to implement on farm. We are not perfect, and nor are we placing pressure on ourselves to be perfect, but we are on a journey towards making our world a better place for our children to grow up in. The following changes are in alphabetical order and in no way the order in which we implemented them.

Agrecovery

Agrecovery provides free recycling for plastic containers from the most common ag-chem, animal health and dairy hygiene products sold into the New Zealand market. All you have to do is remove the lid and triple wash. We use the cage from a thousand-litre IBC pod to store them, and when it's full we take them to our nearest drop-off site (which is at our Farmlands store), where they are inspected and taken for recycling.

Baby wipes

Little packets of baby wipes are so convenient, and I must admit we did use them when out and about with our young girls. But at home we used washcloths, and this really did make a dent in the number of baby wipes we consumed. Those soft little wipes are essentially just little squares of plastic. Now that the girls are older and beyond toilet training, we only need something to wipe hands and faces while away from home. I simply take a face cloth, wet it and wring it dry, then place it in a wet bag with a zip. I can pop it in my purse and use it as we need it.

Bamboo toothbrushes

Here's a scary thought: every plastic toothbrush you've ever owned is still somewhere on the planet. It will never leave.

Our family uses a toothbrush subscription service. Every two months (you can choose how often), our new bamboo toothbrushes arrive in the post in a compostable package, and each toothbrush is individually wrapped in a compostable wrapper. When you discard your old toothbrush you simply snap off the head, or pull the bristles out with pliers, and pop the stick into the compost.

Beauty bars

It started with a sampler pack for Christmas from my sister-in-law, and now I have replaced my shampoo, conditioner, body wash, face cleanser and moisturiser bottles and containers with solid bars. I store my bars in an old soap tin in the bathroom and find they are easy to take on holidays as they take up hardly any space. The girls in fact have never seen a shampoo or body wash plastic bottle in our bathroom, and to them a solid shampoo or body wash bar is just common practice. Most beauty bars come in cardboard and paper packaging to pop in your home compost.

Brass garden fittings

With the extreme temperatures that we get in summer and winter, I find the plastic garden fittings on the hoses and taps don't last much longer than twelve months. It's a waste of money having to replace them so often, and that's not to mention the plastic. I see no need in replacing things that still work, but as the plastic fittings begin to split in the frosts or shatter in the heat, I replace them with brass ones as needed.

Bulk food stores

We are so very lucky that our nearest town has two stores where I can fill up on bulk foods and goods. I gather my empty baking containers and take them to town in a big basket. The shopkeepers weigh the empty containers and I fill them up. Our stores' ranges include any type of flour, baking supply, spice, pasta, grain, seed and nut. I also fill up on golden syrup, honey and cleaning supplies. It's incredible the amount of packaging you can eliminate by filling up at bulk food stores.

Cotton bread bags

Did you know you can store and freeze loaves of bread in 100 per cent cotton/linen bags? They breathe and keep the bread in the dark so it's fresher for longer. I've also sewn a couple of linen tea towels into bags that I use when I make bread, and when I purchase sliced loaves from a bakery. I do, however, continue to purchase plastic bags of bread from the supermarket for farm lunches, and until there's an alternative I am not sure how to avoid this.

Compostable rubbish bags

Despite our best efforts to reduce, reuse and recycle, we still create waste. We use compostable rubbish bags in our home rubbish bins. You do have to be careful not to put anything containing too much moisture in the bin, as this will accelerate the breaking-down process.

Cloth nappies

Both of our girls were in cloth nappies for the majority of the time they needed them. Once you get into a routine of washing, they are quite easy and cost-effective. We weren't perfect though, and used disposables at night (a good night's sleep is hard to argue with when sleep-deprived — we found the disposables kept the girls dry at night for longer) or if we were away on holiday. I used a system of cotton inserts and waterproof covers with snaps, which were adjustable for the girls at different ages. If cloth nappies seem too hard at the moment, then I urge you to consider using a reusable swim nappy. It just goes in the wash with the togs and is packed away for the next visit to the pool. Cloth nappies also mean you always have some on hand (for those who live remotely), and there are no bags of nappies filling up the rubbish bin.

Clothing

When buying new clothing, I have started making conscious decisions to opt for sustainable and natural fabrics. It may mean having to buy fewer items to compensate for the price difference, but good-quality fibres last longer and we are supporting farmers worldwide.

Curtain hooks and sliders

Our bedrooms face south, and in the summer I find the plastic curtain sliders and hooks deteriorate and snap with the constant abuse from the sun. I was replacing them so often that I've decided to swap to roller blinds (with the child-safety tension hooks). There are a couple of other options to consider: stainless-steel curtain hooks and runners, or eyelet curtains that run on a rod.

Dish cloths

I have a collection of cotton dish cloths that I wash regularly, instead of buying disposable ones. See my notes on page 244 about keeping your cotton dish cloths fresh. When they eventually come to the end of their lifespan, just bury them at the bottom of your compost.

Dish brushes

When your plastic dish brush comes to the end of its life, try opting for a wooden one instead. Retire the old plastic one to the laundry for cleaning the dogs' and chickens' water bowls or getting poo off the kids' boots and shoes.

There are many alternatives on the market now — some even have removable heads. If you want more of a stiff brush, coconut fibre ones are ideal for scrubbing. They will of course wear out faster than plastic ones, because you want them to break down (not last on Earth forever). To clean your dish brush, soak it in a solution of warm water and a glug of vinegar before drying fully in sunlight.

Deodorant

I use a deodorant bar instead of an aerosol can or roll-on container. It comes in a cardboard box and I store it in an old soap tin. There are also deodorant sticks and pastes available in cardboard tubes and glass jars. I'm not talking about baking soda homemade options — these bars are effective and smell just as fragrant as your favourite supermarket product.

Drinks in glass bottles or cans

If we are out and about at a café, the lake or up the ski field, we only ever purchase drinks in glass bottles or cans — materials that can be recycled and reused. I like to choose glass bottles that I can repurpose for storing preserves or for bottling chocolate sauce as a gift. If we sit in a café, I will quite often buy only one drink for the small girls and myself. We share the drink between glasses and dilute it with water. It's not only cheaper but also healthier, as fruit drinks often have a lot of sugar in them.

Food scraps

If your food scraps go in an ordinary bin, they end up compacted in a landfill and are denied the oxygen they need to break down. If you are in an urban area your council might provide green bins that are collected for commercial compost, which is fantastic. But here are some other ideas for getting rid of your food scraps. We keep chickens, who pay us back for the food scraps with eggs. We also keep pigs at busy times of the year like shearing, when the chickens can't keep up with the food scraps (we are rewarded with pork for this arrangement). You could get an enclosed compost bin — an open bin such as a pallet bin may attract rats. You could even dig any vegetable and fruit scraps into your garden bed (you don't want to bury any meat, as it will attract flies and smell). Or you could keep aside a bucket for friends who have any of the solutions above.

Fruit and vegetables

I am a novice gardener, but I find growing my own seasonal fruit and vegetables very rewarding. If I do purchase any produce then I like to use:

- **Reusable produce bags**: Just as easy as the change to reusable shopping bags is the change to reusable produce bags such as netted bags. I gift these for birthdays and Christmases so my family and friends have no excuses. If the bags get any marks, I pop them in the washing machine and dry in the sun. I make the conscious choice not to purchase any produce that comes in plastic. I am also that person who takes the grapes out of their plastic bag and puts them into my reusable bag.
- **Fruit subscription services**: I have a standing order with a fruit subscription provider who sends me a variety of seasonal fruit every fortnight. This fruit is produced here in New Zealand and comes in a cardboard box. There are no unnecessary fruit stickers and no plastic packaging.
- **Paper bags for vegetables (such as potatoes)**: I grow a big crop of potatoes each year but, when we run out, I purchase the large five-kilogram paper sacks, avoiding the smaller bags that only come in plastic. The paper bag can then go in the compost.

Glass handwash dispenser

Instead of purchasing a new handwash bottle every time you run out, have you thought of using a glass dispenser or refilling the old bottle? I take a glass bottle to our closest refill station and then top up the dispensers around the house as needed.

Glass spray bottle

I use a glass spray bottle for storing my kitchen spray. I simply refill it with a solution I make (see my citrus-peel recipe in the 'What's up your sleeve?' section). If you don't want to make your own, find a store that sells a refill option. Another idea is to refill the plastic spray bottle you already have until it's no longer useful. It all contributes towards minimising waste.

Home cleaning products

Good marketing has a lot to do with how many plastic bottles of cleaning products are in our households. I encourage you to find one or two cleaning products that can do all the jobs you want and reduce the clutter of products under your laundry sink.

Kitchen items

Quite often people will see items in my kitchen and ask where they can get them, and I have to apologise as I have no idea where they were purchased. A lot of my baking trays, bowls and utensils have been found while fossicking around the old sheds and houses here on the farm. One of my favourite and most well-used appliances is an electric knife that my mum found at a secondhand shop.

I encourage looking for items at secondhand shops, in your old farm shed or by asking family and friends before buying new. Something like a cake tin can be used by several generations and owners, and doesn't need to be new to be useful.

Makeup removal

I use a Norwex makeup cloth to remove my makeup. You simply wet it and wipe your face. It takes off any stubborn mascara too. Alternatively, use crochet cotton makeup pads instead of store-bought single use pads. Simply chuck the Norwex cloth or crochet pads in the wash.

Nappy bags

It doesn't matter what kind of nappies you use, but somehow you have to get them home to either wash or dispose of. You can purchase waterproof nappy bags that seal in the smell and any moisture, and can then be placed in your carrybag without any worries. Just wash with your towels or as you need it again. It might be an idea to buy a few to put in rotation. This will save on the single-use plastic bags that people feel inclined to use for each used nappy.

Postage and courier bags

It's heartening to see new compostable and recyclable postage and courier bags available. I choose either the paper, compostable or dirt bags to send packages, and I'm also proud to support businesses who use these options. I've even been known to wrap parcels in the heavy paper bags that grocery stores are using. All little things to avoid putting more plastic bags into the environment.

Plasback

Silage wrap is unfortunately unavoidable on farm. It is one way to ensure that all of our harvested grass will be consumable for the duration of winter and any dry seasons, when feed is hard to grow for stock. Plasback is a New Zealand company that collects and recycles the wrap to make three products called Tuffboard, Tuffdeck and Plaswood. We buy the large Plasback bags from our local farm store, and at the end of winter we ring Plasback to get them picked up.

Plastic-free Christmas

Last year we asked that all Christmas gifts be plastic-free. It made people really think outside the box, especially as a lot of gifts marketed to children

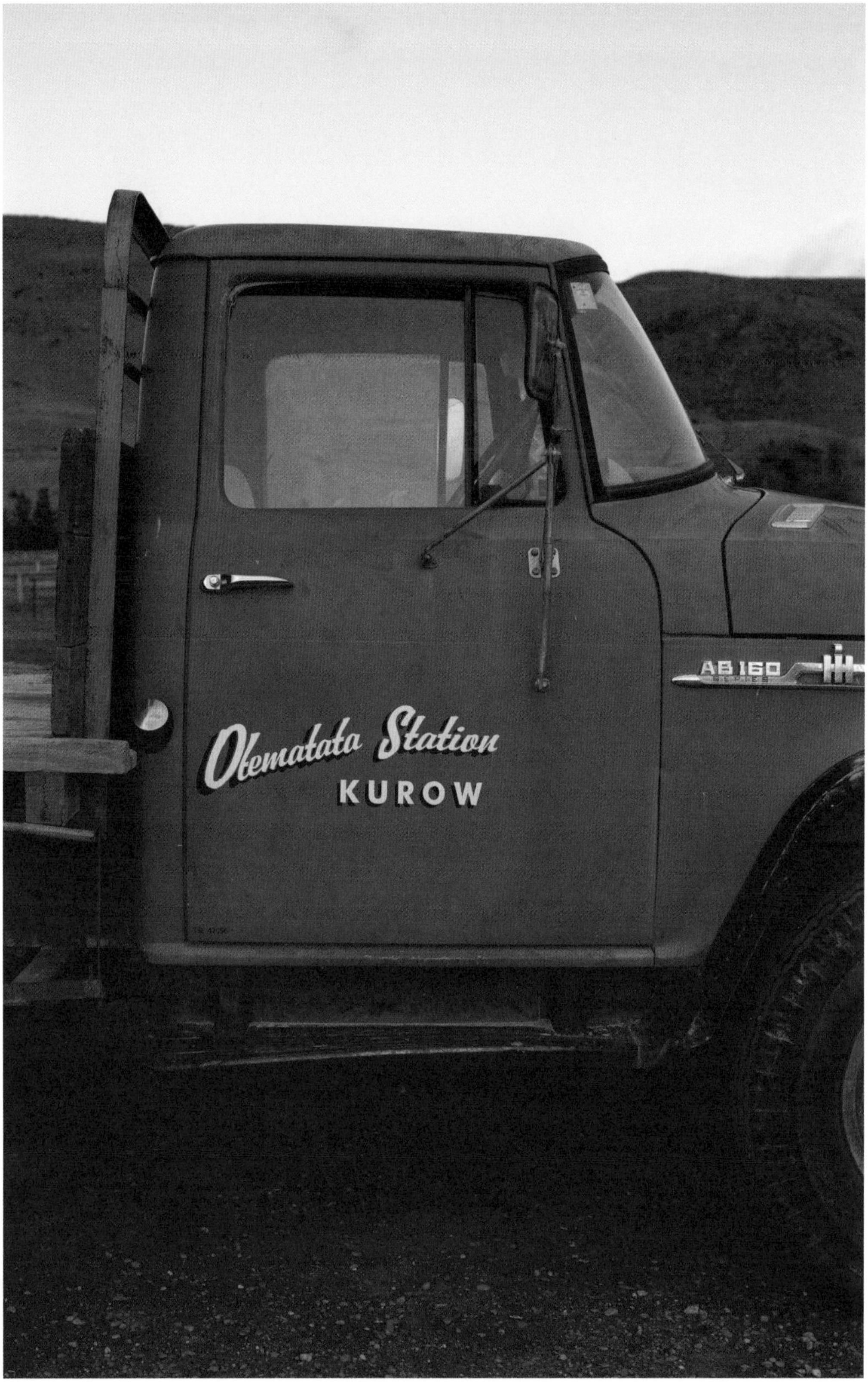
Otematata Station
KUROW
AB 160

are made from unrecyclable parts. What we found was that we ended up supporting small businesses too, who sold fun gifts such as fabric baskets for the girls' bikes or handmade chalk that came in cardboard packaging. My mum made the best gift: a fabric cover that goes over the kitchen table and turns it into a cubby house, complete with windows, a door and little pockets for the girls' books.

Random acts of kindness

Sometimes we need to do one thing not just for the environment, but for other people. Have you heard of Gary Chapman's five love languages? They are: words of affirmation, gifts, acts of service, quality time and physical touch. Every person has a different primary love language that makes their heart smile. I personally relate to acts of service and I love to help others. You may like to give gifts, volunteer, drop in on friends for a cuppa, or perhaps you're a hugger. Whatever it is, if it makes your heart smile then do more of it — you may create a ripple effect, where people pay forward kindness to others.

Recycling on the farm

Since moving to the farm we have actively been introducing recycling into many areas, from the chemical containers and silage wrap, to recycling bins at the shepherds' and shearing quarters. We are lucky that we have a recycling centre not far from the farm gate that takes most types of recycling. The shepherds are responsible for getting their recycling to the centre, and during shearing season we take it down. With clear labelling, there is no excuse for the bins not to be used. This has dramatically reduced our rubbish on farm, and has made staff actively think about what they consider waste.

Reusable baking liners

To avoid using so much baking paper, invest in some reusable baking tray liners. Most good kitchen stores should have some.

Reusable coffee cups

When I have the opportunity to get a great coffee off farm, I make the most of it. Over a year ago I decided that I would either have to sit in more, or use a reusable cup for takeaway. No reusable cup, no coffee. I've only forgotten it once. There is even a café in Oamaru that rewards you for using a reusable cup with two stamps on your loyalty card. Now that's some marketing I can buy into.

Reusable shopping bags

New Zealand has banned single-use shopping bags since July 2019, which is great. But unless you regularly remember to take in your reusable bags, we are still creating unnecessary waste by having to purchase either paper or cloth bags. I recently read that a reusable bag must be used between five and 50 times (depending on the fabric) to offset the climate change impact from manufacturing. So it's important to remember to use your stash of bags rather than contribute more to the pile. This is not to say that I haven't had to purchase a few bags at a pinch, but the fact that we are consciously changing our behaviour is what matters.

Reusable razors

I have been using a reusable stainless-steel safety razor now for over a year. I made the choice to swap when my last plastic disposable razor refill was used. It takes one or two times to get used to using it, as there is no protection from the blade like in a lot of the products at the grocery store, but once you do, the smooth shave is unbeatable. There are a lot of companies with this product on offer now, and I chose one where I can return my blades to be recycled into scrap metal.

School lunches

Since Flora has started school she has begun to see the variety of fun packaged foods that some families buy. She understands why we don't purchase foods with excessive packaging, but it's not easy for her to see friends with *Paw Patrol* cookies while hers are home-baked. Here are some of the ways we try to eliminate waste and packaging with school lunches.

- **Stainless-steel lunchboxes**: We have a simple stainless-steel lunchbox with three compartments. It's great for separating items and eliminating wrapping, but it's also a hardy material that won't break or crack like plastic, meaning it's cost-efficient in the longterm. I can see these lunchboxes lasting a lifetime at school. You can purchase fun decals or stickers to cover them with your kid's favourite character this month, and if for some reason they were to get crushed or damaged, they can be dropped at your nearest scrap metal dealership and have another life.

- **Beeswax wraps**: We use beeswax wraps instead of clingfilm. There are plenty of people selling these online or at little markets. Fun patterns can liven up the lunchbox.

- **Stainless-steel flasks**: These are great for taking leftovers to school and keeping food warm.

- **Stainless-steel drink bottles**: There are so many cost-effective stainless-steel drink bottles for sale now. The thing I love about these is that they can hit the concrete in the playground and, although they may have a dent, they will stand the test of time for many more years.

- **Sandwich pouches**: I found the girls some fabulous sandwich pouches at a little stall at the Waimate Strawberry Fare. They are material pouches lined with a wipeable fabric, and can be sealed with a Velcro strip. Each night I wipe them out and they are good to be used the next day again. They keep sandwiches just as fresh as they would be wrapped in clingfilm.

- **Silicone and reusable yoghurt pouches**: Once again there are plenty of these on the market, and I'm sure you will find some at any kitchen store or with a quick Google search. We make our own yoghurt and fill the pouches each morning. When they come home we simply wash them in hot, soapy water and use again. They are great for smoothies and can be frozen too.

Shaving bars

Joe received a shaving bar last year for our plastic-free Christmas. It's replaced his usual can of shaving foam, and he's blown away with how efficient it is. It smells incredible, is soft on the skin, and he reckons it gives him a better shave.

Silicone food covers for the fridge

Silicone food covers come in several sizes and stretch over any round bowl. This eliminates any need for clingfilm and they can be easily washed in hot, soapy water to be used again.

Soap

I have ditched bottles of body wash in the shower for two reasons: I needed a nylon mesh shower puff to lather up the liquid, and the packaging was unnecessary. I've gone back to a bar of soap. It does contribute to scum on the shower glass, but I simply have a scrubby cloth in the shower and wipe down the glass every now and then to stop the build-up.

Stainless-steel pegs

As the last of my plastic pegs begin to snap in the summer heat and from plenty of use, I'm beginning to replace them with stainless-steel pegs. They are a lot gentler on softer fabrics like merino too. I've gathered my wee stash of stainless-steel pegs from school fundraisers and online deals.

Sweets in paper or cardboard packaging

The sweets aisles at the supermarket or in the dairy are littered with single-use packaging. I make a conscious choice only to purchase the ones in cardboard or compostable packaging. This also makes me think twice about whether I need to purchase the treat in the first place.

Swimming bags

We use fabric wet bags for carrying home our swimming togs and towels. Growing up we would have used a supermarket plastic bag and thrown it away after ripping it open because we couldn't untie our own knots. I just empty the wet bag into the washing machine and dump the wet bag in there too. They dry just as quickly as a pair of togs, so are good to go again the next day.

Toilet paper and paper towel subscriptions

There are a few toilet paper and paper towel subscriptions available online, and a lot of them are using bamboo, which is faster-growing than the traditional woods used in paper. You can choose the amount and frequency in which they arrive, but the best part is that there is no plastic wrap, no fragrance (which means no unnecessary chemicals) and the wrapping is compostable at home.

Wendyl Nissen

Not long after Joe and I married, my good friend Jane Millton gave me a copy of Wendyl Nissen's book *Mother's Little Helper*, knowing that we would start a family one day. I read it from cover to cover and it still sits on my bedside table. The pages are well thumbed and the corners turned down on the most helpful pages. It made me look at our home and think about what was important. Nissen has sensible suggestions for using secondhand items and simplifying what you need for a baby, rather than getting caught up in all the marketing. It is one of my favourite books to gift or recommend to friends. Her 2018 book *The Natural Home* covers similar topics and more.

Yoghurt

We love yoghurt in our house, but most come in a Code 5 plastic pottle, which we can no longer recycle in our area — we are restricted to Codes 1 and 2. Instead of buying store-bought yoghurt, we have been making our own.

The majority of the time we make yoghurt using a yogurt-maker. There are so many plastic insulated yoghurt-makers to be found in secondhand shops around the country that there is no need to purchase a new one. I see there are now stainless-steel varieties too, and companies are beginning to offer better packaging for their cultures.

In addition to these packet yoghurts, we've been experimenting with making our own yoghurt in the magic pot (multicooker), though we are still perfecting that process. One important tip we have learnt so far is to wipe the pot with white vinegar to eliminate any tainting flavours from the last meal cooked.

Recipe index

Gratitude

THANK YOU TO THOSE OF YOU who have helped me with my Instagram journey. Without you, this opportunity to share my stories and recipes would never have existed:

Laura MacDonald @thekiwicountrygirl

Vanya Insull @vj_cooks

Anna Cameron @justamumnz

Jana MacPherson @the_macpherson_diaries

Thank you to Jenny Hellen, Publishing Director at Allen & Unwin New Zealand, who had the idea to document our life here in Otematata. What an opportunity! Thanks also to the A&U team, including Leanne McGregor, Abba Renshaw and Courtney Smith, freelance editors Holly Hunter and Síana Clifford, designer Kate Barraclough and proofreaders Kate Stone and Cassie Doherty.

Thank you to the recipe testers: Jane Egden, Jane Millton, Cherie Matheson, Sarah Paterson, Olivia Hawke, Leigh Fodie, Ruth Smallwood and Jess Brown. You helped in so many ways with your words of encouragement and kindly worded reviews.

Thank you to Dana Johnston for the year of adventures photographing this life of ours. It was tricky to capture a whole year while we spent a majority of it in lockdown — but we got there.

Thank you to our new friend Lottie Hedley, who took those mouth-watering photographs of all the recipes and our wee family. You know you are always welcome here. I'll grab a bottle of red for when you arrive.

Thank you to talented photographer Derek Morrison, whose kindness goes beyond generous, and to Aaron Smale for the merino photograph.

Thank you to Franny for your sensational light-umbrella-holding skills, and to Nick, whose dogs were well behaved (despite not making the cover shot). Thank you to Charlotte Calder — you are not only a great hand model, but you were fantastic with our girls. Thank you to my talented friend Emma Nowell, who sketched the baking paper techniques. You understood my ramblings and brought my vague words to life.

Thank you to my father-in-law, Hugh, who helped fill my knowledge gaps in the farm's history. It is you who needs to write a book next.

Thank you to Mum for helping with the girls, with the pick-ups and the drop-offs. I know you three were all having a good time, but I really do appreciate the kilometres travelled and hours at the library.

Lastly I would like to thank my Joe, who encouraged me to write this book from when it was first discussed. You encourage me and inspire me like no other. You are my mallard and I do appreciate everything you do for our family and me. We are a team, and I believe pretty bloody awesome parents to our two little humans.

Image credits

© Dana Johnston: case spine and pages 2, 8, 10, 13, 20, 23, 24, 30, 32, 37, 40, 43, 48, 51, 55, 58 (top right), 60, 62, 80, 82, 83, 85, 89, 92, 95, 96, 102, 105, 106, 112, 116, 119, 124, 130, 137, 141, 145, 149, 150, 152, 159, 163, 164, 168, 171, 185, 236, 239 (top left and right), 246 (bottom), 258, 262, 267, 277, 280 and 288

© Lottie Hedley: front cover, back cover and pages 4, 6, 7, 16, 26, 29, 58 (top left and bottom), 65, 67, 69, 71, 73, 75, 77, 79, 101, 115, 123, 127, 129, 133, 135, 139, 143, 147, 172, 177, 179, 181, 183, 187, 189, 191, 193, 195, 196, 198, 203, 207, 208, 212, 214, 217, 219, 221, 223, 225, 227, 229, 231, 233, 234, 239 (bottom), 241, 242, 245, 246 (top left and right), 249, 250, 257, 272, 284 and 287

© Derek Morrison: page 174

© Aaron Smale: page 155

© Emma Nowell: illustrations on pages 252–254

Historical photographs on pages 19, 33, 38, 39, 46, 91, 109, 111 and 153 are from Philippa Cameron's family collection. Thanks to Deirdre Sisson (nee Lousley) for the historical photograph on page 83.

First published in 2021

Text © Philippa Cameron 2021
Photography © Dana Johnston and Lottie Hedley 2021, unless
otherwise credited (see page 286)

Allen & Unwin
Level 2, 10 College Hill, Freemans Bay
Auckland 1011, New Zealand
Phone: (64 9) 377 3800
Email: auckland@allenandunwin.com
Web: www.allenandunwin.co.nz

83 Alexander Street
Crows Nest NSW 2065, Australia
Phone: (61 2) 8425 0100

A catalogue record for this book is available from the
National Library of New Zealand.

ISBN 978 1 98854 747 3

Design by Kate Barraclough
Set in Adobe Caslon Pro, Domaine Display and Brandon Text
Printed in China by C & C Offset Printing Co., Ltd.

5 7 9 10 8 6 4

FSC
www.fsc.org

MIX
Paper from
responsible sources
FSC® C008047